About the Author

Sharon Dilley has been an animal lover since she was a child and has enjoyed many dogs in her life. She has also been an elementary teacher, specializing in early childhood education for many years. The teaching process that she followed with children over the years helped her create the training program she now uses with the dogs.

Young children and young dogs are not all that different in the ways they learn. She noticed that the strategies she used to help children learn and grow in confidence and autonomy were easily transferable to the dogs she was partnering with. She'll be sharing those learning strategies with you throughout the pages of this book.

She has worked with dogs in a wide variety of disciplines,

including search and rescue, therapy dog training, and service dog training. She has worked with rescue organizations and pet parents. Her ultimate goal in all of these scenarios is to provide the people and dogs with the knowledge and skills to enjoy the journey through life together. The combination of being a disaster search and rescue handler and having years of teaching experience has impacted her approach to how she teaches, trains and supports dogs to be secure, self-regulated, well-mannered, and happy as they navigate the complex and often confusing human world.

Over the course of many years, with much trial and error and with the spectacular patience of so many wonderful dogs, she developed a methodology of teaching, guidance, support, and partnership that helps dogs reach their maximum potential. One that teaches them manners and life skills as they learn how to navigate the crazy human world. This approach provides them with the opportunity to maximize their strengths and develop independent confidence as they grow into their jobs.

Her intention through sharing personal insights, a few of the many mistakes she has made, and a wide variety of training tips and practices is that you too will be able to develop an understanding of your dog which will complement your current training program. Her goal is for you to learn how to partner with your canine friend in such a way that supports them and provides them with excellent foundation that will positively impact your current training program.

The Puppy Puzzle

Sharon Dilley

The Puppy Puzzle

Olympia Publishers
London

www.olympiapublishers.com
OLYMPIA PAPERBACK EDITION

Copyright © Sharon Dilley 2024

The right of Sharon Dilley to be identified as author of
this work has been asserted in accordance with sections 77 and 78 of
the Copyright, Designs and Patents Act 1988.

All Rights Reserved

No reproduction, copy or transmission of this publication
may be made without written permission.
No paragraph of this publication may be reproduced,
copied or transmitted save with the written permission of the publisher,
or in accordance with the provisions
of the Copyright Act 1956 (as amended).

Any person who commits any unauthorized act in relation to
this publication may be liable to criminal
prosecution and civil claims for damage.

A CIP catalogue record for this title is
available from the British Library.

ISBN: 978-1-80439-614-8

The information in this book has been compiled by way of general
guidance only. Neither the author nor the publisher shall be liable or
responsible for any loss or damage allegedly arising from any
information or suggestion in this book.

First Published in 2024

Olympia Publishers
Tallis House
2 Tallis Street
London
EC4Y 0AB

Printed in Great Britain

Dedication

I dedicate *The Puppy Puzzle* to my husband, John. His encouragement, guidance and support have been unwavering since I started writing. Without him *The Puppy Puzzle* would not have been born. Thank you!

Acknowledgments

The journey of bringing this book to fruition has been a deeply rewarding process, one that I could not have created on my own. I am eternally grateful to every trainer I've ever interacted with. I have learned from each one of you.

I'd like to thank the many FEMA and Urban Search and Rescue Task Force members, Firefighters and other Emergency teams across the country who taught, inspired and supported me as I developed my skills and deepened my understanding of Search and Rescue. For me, it's where it all began.

I want to extend a special thank you to the USAR team in Oklahoma: Dane Yaw, Jason Smith, Brent Koeninger, Mark Edwards, Chet Clark, Justin Leachman, and Andrew McCann for teaching me so much. And to the Kansas USAR team, Randy Hill, Sheila Stern, Heather Jones and countless others who demonstrate unwavering dedication to finding the missing or buried under the rubble. I have learned from each and every one of you.

Thank you Simone Wright for diligently working with me and encouraging me to FINISH!

A special thank you to Dr. Robin Ganzert, Jack Hubbard and Dr. Amy Hrin with American Humane for believing in my abilities as a service dog trainer and providing a way for me to live my passion.

And to all the veterans I have ever had the privilege to work with, thank you for your service to our great country!

Introduction

"So many times, we underestimate our dogs. They know more than we give them credit for."

– Sharon Dilley

The desire of most people who live and work with dogs is universal. That is to live our best life with our dogs, to enjoy the connection with them and teach them manners and life skills to navigate the human world. For those who train search and rescue dogs, detection dogs, service dogs, therapy dogs, agility dogs, etc. the goal is to maximize the dog's potential, helping them be the best they can be.

The challenge most of us face when working with dogs in any discipline is, how can we train them in a way that encourages them to reach their maximum potential? For dog parents who simply want to live and enjoy life with their dogs, how can we efficiently teach the life skills and manners to make life with our buddy a little smoother? For search and rescue dogs, how can we teach them to be just a little more effective when finding the lost human? For service dogs, how can we teach them in a way that allows independence to make decisions to best help their veteran or handler? And for working dogs, how can we teach the dogs in a way that expands their potential just enough to give them an edge in their chosen profession when lives may be at risk?

Basically, how can we create a scenario where the dog both learns the job we chose for them and thrives at the same time? Once we figure that out, how can we create a training program to teach necessary skills while meeting the dog's needs to just be a dog?

I have spent many years of my adult life looking for that perfect balance…

I am a lifelong learner who questions myself and my training methods in an effort to constantly improve.

What would happen if we encouraged independent thinking and allowed our dogs the freedom to make choices on as many of their behaviors as possible? Would they be more receptive and be able to learn and integrate behaviors without so much drilling? Could we acknowledge and capture the moment of choice to teach them the manners and life skills more quickly?

These questions opened a new pathway through which I started traveling with my dogs. Along the way I discovered that many of the things I pondered could be answered by the three fundamental Puzzle Pieces I introduce in the following pages.

PUTTING THE PIECES TOGETHER

I noticed that the strategies to make these outcomes easily evident, all began to fit together like a unique and living puzzle. And just like putting an actual puzzle together, you need to know what the image is you are working with in order to have an idea about where to begin.

I knew I wanted my dogs to be happy, well adjusted, secure and confident. That became my starting point. Over time, the pieces of the puzzle that were necessary to develop a training program that taught the desired skills while allowing the dog to simply be a dog began to fall into place.

Eventually a simple formula began to emerge that when applied consistently resulted in the puppies and dogs learning and retaining new information more quickly than ever before. And as an additional bonus, I noticed how even many troublesome behaviors were beginning to disappear as the dogs progressed. They began to recognize the power of their choices. When dogs realize they have choices and their choices impact their life, the learning happens at an astounding rate.

The process I call 'The Puppy Puzzle' has the ability to complement every training program in any discipline and is the foundation of how I work with every dog that crosses my path. When applied consistently, 'The Puppy Puzzle' has the power to change your life and help your dog THRIVE like never before! I am honored to share it with you now.

PART 1

THE PIECES OF THE PUPPY PUZZLE

CONNECTION, MEETING YOUR DOG'S NEEDS AND REGULATING THE ENVIRONMENT

CHAPTER 1

THE PIECES OF THE PUPPY PUZZLE

"Just because a puzzle is in pieces doesn't mean it's broken. It's just waiting to be put together."

– John Dilley

Teaching our dogs the life skills and manners they need to thrive does not need to be complicated. The framework of The Puppy Puzzle is imbedded within the THREE IMPORTANT and FOUNDATIONAL PIECES;

CONNECTION
MEETING NEEDS
REGULATING THE ENVIRONMENT

When you think about how a puzzle is assembled, you understand that each piece is valuable and indispensable to the complete picture. You know as well that the pieces are designed to fit together easily.

This is the same understanding we bring to The Puppy Puzzle. Each of the three pieces is an important element individually and contains important information within it. Each puzzle piece is valuable on its own, and I invite you to practice with each of them as separate pieces, but it is when they are all integrated and fit together as a complete picture that the power really starts to make a difference in your dog's life. And both you and your pup benefit!

In this chapter I provide a brief description of what each of The Puzzle Pieces are and how they will give you an advantage when working with your dog. In the following chapters, we'll dive deeper into the elements of each and I'll provide you with tips and practice exercises to help you expand your knowledge and enrich your training.

PIECE 1: CONNECTION

The first Puzzle Piece to incorporate into your current training program is CONNECTION. This engagement applies to dogs of all ages and is the first Puzzle Piece to creating an incredible partnership. Whether you're starting with a young puppy or a more mature dog, this piece will enhance your current training plan. CONNECTION is crucial at any age and stage of development and is the first piece of The Puppy Puzzle. Connection simply means to becomes your pup's best friend.

I like to call it, 'Being more fun than dirt.' The type of relationship where YOU become the best thing in your dog's life, where you develop a partnership that promotes trust in you, learning and working together with ease.

Connection happens when you become the focal point of your dog's affection and attention. You become their North Star, their Guiding Light and Ultimate Mentor. Your dog wants and needs you to be these things for him, so he can develop trust in you that grows into an unshakable bond.

PIECE 2: MEETING YOUR DOG'S NEEDS

The second Puzzle Piece is MEETING YOUR DOG'S NEEDS. This piece requires more awareness from you as you begin to anticipate what your dog needs. After you realize what your dog's needs are, you strive to meet those needs before they have to advocate for themselves. This builds the trust in you.

The needs we are talking about are not only the basics of food, water, shelter and safety. But also, the needs to be a happy, settled dog, the needs of sniffing, digging, chewing, playing, exercise, rest and interaction with people and other dogs. Simply put, providing time and space for your dog to be a dog and do the things he loves to do.

When NEEDS are met in any creature, (humans included) the organism moves from the limitation of surviving into the endless potential of thriving. This is the place we want our dogs to be in order for them to learn and grow into their maximum potential.

PIECE 3: REGULATING THE ENVIRONMENT

The last Puzzle Piece is regulating the environment until the pup learns to regulate themselves.

REGULATING THE ENVIRONMENT means to refine the environment in which you and your dog are practicing to a point where the dog experiences success. It means to set up the surroundings in such a way that you give the dog an opportunity to choose his behavior correctly and then reward his choice by saying, "YES! That's exactly what I need you to do in this moment."

As you learn how to set up the ENVIRONMENT to ensure your dog's success, your dog learns what choices benefit him the most. Dogs are simple creatures and do what works for them. They are very smart in figuring out how to get what they want. Setting up the environment for success allows your dog to develop more confidence in themselves and learn incredible life skills to navigate the human world and excel in their chosen job.

Success in any area of life is rarely an accident. REGULATING THE ENVIRONMENT, prepares you and your dog to be successful, ahead of time.

At home, 'Regulating the Environment' might mean keeping your young puppy on a leash, so you don't miss the signs of needing to go out to use the bathroom. Or it may look like you blocking off parts of your home, so the little one doesn't chew on things he is not supposed to. It may also mean using the kennel when appropriate or providing distance from 'scary' things when out on walks, etc.

Implementing the regulation of the environment is one of the pieces of The Puppy Puzzle that will relax as time passes and your dog learns manners and life skills or his chosen job. When their behaviors become so proficient, they are able to navigate their surrounding with ease and efficiency, you will be able to relax and enjoy more freedom with your pup.

THE ULTIMATE EQUATION

The three simple yet powerful pieces of The Puppy Puzzle help you create an amazing formula for success. As easy as 1, 2, 3. The elements of Connection + Meeting the Dog's Needs + Regulating the Environment = One Happy Successful Dog.

As this process becomes more natural, you'll learn how to Capture all of the wonderful behaviors your pup exhibits every day, so they become automatic life skills.

You'll also develop the skills and know how to Ignore, Interrupt, Replace and Reset undesired behaviors, so they do not become habits that make life more difficult.

As you become fluent with each piece of The Puppy Puzzle, you'll develop a deeper and more dynamic relationship with your dog. Like a school of fish that move together to avoid becoming prey for larger fish, you and your dog will have the ability to communicate without speaking, to engage without struggle and know precisely how to move through life together. If you have a working dog, competition dog, service dog or pet dog, the benefits are life changing.

The result is a harmonious partnership, a well-mannered and secure dog, eager to learn and do their job in this life. The discipline you and your pup choose is irrelevant. If you desire a snuggle buddy, a service dog, therapy dog, search and rescue, detection, agility, hunt dog or anything else, the THREE PIECES of THE PUPPY PUZZLE will benefit your current training program.

PRE-PRACTICE PROTOCOLS

Throughout The Puppy Puzzle I'll be providing you with Practice exercises.

Prior to starting any Practice, please meet your dog's needs. Allow time and space to use the bathroom and expend some of his endless energy. Focus is very difficult when they are hungry, need to run or need to use the bathroom.

Also remind yourself as you navigate these learning protocols, that your dog does not do things to frustrate you, nor are they being stubborn. If you find yourself stuck and your dog is not behaving as expected, instead of looking to your dog as the problem, realize they are giving you information. Figure it out. I invite you instead, to ask yourself, "What is my dog communicating and how can I do things differently to set them up for success?" Notice when something is off or not working, re-evaluate YOUR plans and change your training plan.

Check your emotions at the door. Remain neutral when interacting with your dog and you will discover how to move them through challenging situations much easier.

It is my heartfelt intention that the skills you will learn in the pages of this book set you and your dog up for a lifetime of learning together, joy, and success.

Now, let's go have some fun and start putting the pieces together.

CHAPTER 2

CONNECTION

"Be your dog's best buddy!"

– John Dilley

Encouraging a powerful CONNECTION with your dog is the framework of The Puppy Puzzle that provides you with the stability and foundation on which your success will be built. It is the first piece of The Puppy Puzzle.

As you develop CONNECTION with your dog, your ability to teach manners, life skills and their chosen job becomes like a dance. You are the partner who 'leads' and your pup follows, ultimately working together to the point where you can navigate the life together beautifully.

Every single interaction, especially in the beginning, has the power to enhance the budding relationship or inhibit it. Take the time in the beginning to notice the tiny little details of your dog's personality, his character traits, his natural abilities, his preferences and his limitations. This is the time to build trust. It is a time when they begin believing that you are their number one advocate and that you always have their best interests at the center of your training. It is a crucial time as you begin teaching skills.

It is also important to remember, just as YOU are getting to know THEM… they are getting to know YOU. CONNECTION is a two-way street, pay attention to their body language and what they are communicating. Set them up for success by listening and responding as you figure out how to work together.

Dogs are incredibly brilliant, perceptive creatures. They figure out very quickly which behaviors benefit them and which behaviors elicit negative consequences. They notice your tone of voice, facial expressions, and your body language and adapt accordingly to get what they want out of life.

CONNECTION: is the piece of the puzzle where two-way communication becomes more and more important. Now is the time for you to pay attention to them in order to respond quickly to what they are attempting to tell you. Whether you have a pet dog, agility dog, service dog, detection dog or search and rescue dog, the benefits of a strong reliable connection will maximize their potential. It will help you navigate the simple and the challenging moments.

When you invest the time in creating a relationship built on trust, reliability and taking care of each other, the daily challenges become another day in your partnership as you journey together through life.

PIPER: JOHN'S SURGERY AND MY SPECTACULAR ERROR

Some years ago, my husband, John, had neck surgery. On our arrival home, our dogs were excited to have him back. John and Piper have a fun greeting ritual where she jumps toward him, and he 'catches her mid air' and pets her back to the ground.

To prevent any sort of jostling of John's neck, I attached a leash to Piper to prevent her from jumping into the middle of him and allow them a more subdued greeting.

A short time later, when things had settled and I let Piper off the leash, she bolted away from me and straight to John who was resting in his chair. She planned to give him a proper greeting right in the face like she always did. This moment for Piper was no different than any other and to her, the normal rules applied.

Before she could get very far, I grabbed Piper's collar and said a firm and strong "No." Much more harshly than normal.

The thought of Piper accidentally hurting John in his vulnerable state scared me and the fear came through my voice.

To avoid Piper accidentally hurting John, I secured all of the dogs on the back porch where they were free to come and go, in and out, but didn't have access to John. At this point, it had only been twenty-four hours since his surgery and I was not thinking about training dogs or how my actions would negatively affect Piper.

The next few days were a blur of taking care of John and keeping the dogs separated from him for his protection. The dogs love John, but they are rough, and he is their favorite toy. Piper also loves sitting in his chair with him (again something they have done since she was a tiny puppy) and the only way to prevent her from jumping into his lap was to keep her out of the living area.

A couple of days after his surgery, John was feeling much better and was ready to spend some time with Piper. I let her in the room, and she rushed past me to the front door so she could go outside to play.

I sat beside John and called her to us, but she refused to come and eventually bolted to the back bedroom. I found her and gently took a hold of her collar, placed a leash on her to bring her to John. She absolutely refused!

She laid down, barked and growled at me, effectively telling me, "No, I am not going near him." I knew immediately how my actions had negatively affected her. I had broken two very powerful connection rules: I had scolded her and isolated her. Her trust in me, in that moment was broken.

I grabbed a clicker and some treats and sat near John. I invited Piper to come to us. Every time she took a step closer to John, I clicked and tossed her a treat. Piper finally walked to

John, sat in front of his chair and leaned in close so he could reach her. With the bond now re-established, Piper could sense that John wasn't feeling 100% and she calmed her normally rowdy behavior to accommodate his tender state.

In the following days, Piper modified her own behavior changing from boisterous playmate to diligent protector. Even intercepting attempts from the other dogs to interact with him. It was an incredible moment to witness.

As I reflected on my actions in the early days of John's recovery, I realized the magnitude of trust I broke with Piper that day. Not only did I scold her, possibly for the first time in her life, I isolated her from her favorite humans.

Isolation is a HUGE punishment. Even though she was with the other dogs, had bones to chew and complete access to the outside, it didn't matter because she was separated from us, her people. This was a shock to Piper, and it destabilized her trust in me. Because her connection with me was well established and the foundation of our relationship strong, I was able to repair the damage very quickly.

CONNECTION IS CRUCIAL

The relationship you create with your dog is possibly the most important piece of the Puppy Puzzle, which is why it is #1 in the framework of the puzzle. The bond and trust are vital to every other piece of the puzzle.

It's important to remember that when you begin a new life with your pup, EVERYTHING is different for them. These early days can be tough, because the environment that was once familiar has now been replaced with a stranger and different surroundings.

In the first hours, days, weeks, I invite you to make CONNECTION your number one priority. Spend time together with zero expectations. Enjoy your dog, play with them, feed them, love on them and notice what they are telling you. Simply allow them to be who they are.

Take long walks, not to train, teach or correct anything, but simply to get to know one another. Allow time for them to become familiar with the environment that is now 'home.' There will be plenty of time to teach them their job and the life skills needed to thrive in the human world later.

Create the opportunity in these early days to establish the CONNECTION that builds the trust in you and deepens the knowledge within them, that *you* will take care of their needs and be their advocate.

As you show them you are their advocate, that you are dependable, and will guide them while giving them the flexibility and autonomy to make choices for themselves; you become irresistible. You become the leader they want to partner with… and they choose you!

Once they choose you, you have IT! You have their attention and when you have their attention, the possibilities of what you can accomplish together are endless.

PRACTICE: PLAY BREAKS

Life skill: Play Breaks are a powerful way of increasing your dog's focus on you while decreasing their attention of their surroundings. Taking a Play Break builds connection with you. This practice regulates the environment naturally, because distractions that pull attention pale in comparison to the fun and interaction generated by you.

Puzzle Pieces for Success

Piece 1: Movement from your dog.

Piece 2: Interaction with you.

Piece 3: Keep it short. 2–3 minutes maximum.

Supplies: A human willing to move and get excited, a dog (on the leash), tug toys, and a small space. I use this game when training service dogs in public to relieve stress and provide fun during the 'work' day.

Putting the Pieces Together

Step 1: Begin with your dog on leash in a quiet out of the way area. If I'm in a store, I find a quiet aisle where there are few people.

Step 2: Engage with your dog. At this point, show them the tug toy. Tap the floor on your right, then tap on your left, very quickly allowing the dog enough leash to move freely and chase it while you move it. When outside, use a high-pitched voice, when inside and you need to be quiet, use a voice little more than a whisper, but talking very fast. Increase your energy and your pup will respond.

TIP: If your pup is totally uninterested in toys, use treats or a squeaker or clicker or even just YOU. Whatever gets your dog excited and perks up his ears. Regardless of what you choose, the action must keep the dog *engaged with you, focused on you and moving.*

Step 3: Play tug, jog back and forth, make eye contact, pat your pup on his side and interact with him.

TIP: Your pup needs to be in motion tugging, running or playing the entire time with their focus on you. Do NOT play ball, because then the dog is engaging with the ball and not with you.

Step 4: Stop the play and notice what your pup is doing. Is he looking directly at you ready for more? If the answer is yes, you have played enough and may resume the task at hand. If they immediately look around or sniff the floor/ground, you need to repeat the steps and raise your energy up another level. Become super exciting.

TIP: Notice their interest in you, their natural engagement and willingness to focus on you. Remember, you want to be 'More FUN than dirt!'

Step 5: Go back to what you were doing before you took a Play Break and notice the difference in your dog. Do the distractions that previously captured your dog's attention become less of an issue? If so, consider the practice a success. If not, try it again with a little more enthusiasm.

PIPER: JUST OUT OF REACH

Piper loves to play tug more than anything. One of the elements of training a search and rescue dog, and acknowledging a successful outcome is a game of tug with the person she found. This becomes a reward and a much-appreciated way of saying, "YES, you found me! Good dog! That is exactly what you need to do!"

The challenge I encountered with Piper early on (between the ages of five and nine months) was the fact she chewed any toy up that I allowed her to keep for any length of time.

She had a favorite toy we used as her reward when she found the hidden person, they played with her and I promptly took her toy and put it away for safe keeping... until our next practice run. From my point of view, I was preserving her favorite toy for future use. From Piper's point of view, I was keeping the prize she worked for. In her mind, I stole it.

Before long, after a few more of these toy violations on my part, she didn't come all the way back to me. Instead, she laid down with her toy, just beyond my reach. When I moved toward her, she moved a little further away.

I realized how my actions had unintentionally created the behavior of her positioning herself in such a way that I could not limit the enjoyment of her rightfully earned reward. My actions broke Piper's trust in an unspoken agreement that if I do this thing correctly for you human, I get to play with my toy. I had broken the deal and she lost trust in me.

This lesson redefined two fundamental rules of Connection I now live by:
1. NEVER take something from them! Trade them instead.
2. Be the FUN, not the fun killer.

DEEPENING TRUST

Your actions from the moment you bring your dog home affects every aspect of their behavior and creates the level of trust they either have, or don't have in you. It becomes an equation of 'what you put in is what you get out.' And, 'how well you respond to what they are telling you determines the outcome of the challenge.' Their behavior becomes a reflection of your interactions with them.

As you move through life supporting your pup, their capacity to learn will grow, because their trust in you will grow.

Below are some of the elements I have consistently practiced to encourage Connection and Trust:

- Allow dogs the freedom to make choices in as many areas of their life as possible.
- Create predictable positive interactions with humans.
- Advocate for and protect your dog at all times. Trust your instincts.
- Provide a safe, quiet place to rest.
- Be consistent (regular nutritious meals, dependable schedules etc.)
- Provide plenty of puppy play time, outside time, and human time.

- Very little kennel time, especially in the beginning.
- Regulate their environment until they have the ability to regulate themselves.

A few practices that hinder trust are:

- Not enough time to do dog stuff, i.e.: sniffing, chewing, running and playing.
- Social isolation. Too much time in the kennel.
- Scolding or unpredictable reactions from important humans.
- No response or a negative response when they express need.
- Not enough family or human time.
- Not enough time allowed to run and play.
- Not enough fun or exciting things to do/too little enrichment.

These trust builders and trust breakers may seem simple, but they are vital when you're building the Connection piece of the puzzle. So, while these details may seem minor, they will pay major dividends when applied correctly.

YOUR ACTIONS IMPACT YOUR DOG'S BEHAVIOR

When you start witnessing a behavior that is out of character or different from previous behaviors, think about your actions immediately preceding the behavior or immediately following the behavior.

For example: when you take your dog out to go to the bathroom, he goes quickly, and you immediately take him back inside. Before long when you take him out, he sniffs, and sniffs and sniffs some more before finally deciding on a spot worthy to do his business.

Your action of immediately taking him inside after he goes to the bathroom has a direct impact on how quickly he goes in the future. You did not allow him time to sniff his world before. Now your dog becomes his own advocate and will take his sniffing time prior to going to the bathroom. Dogs are incredible at taking advantage of situations to ensure their own needs are met if you do not proactively meet their needs.

I invite you to make a list of your dog's behaviors that are less than ideal. For example: Is he slow to come when called or ignoring you altogether? Is he begging when humans are eating, or jumping on you when you walk in the door?

Now think about *your* actions immediately preceding or immediately following those behaviors. What are you doing or what have you previously done to encourage it?

- When your pup is slow to come, are you the fun killer? Do they have to go inside or stop playing after you call them?

- How many times have you given your dog food when dining immediately after they whined or begged?
- When your dog jumps, how much attention are they getting with their paws in your middle? They simply want to greet you, bend down and greet them while their paws are on the ground.

You get the idea. We are creating our dog's behaviors through our interactions with them and the timing of our interactions with them. We want to be sure we are setting them up for as much success as possible. Awareness of our own behavior is very important when interacting with our dogs.

PRACTICE: GREETINGS WITH 4 PAWS ON THE FLOOR

Life skill: This practice teaches the dog that you will meet their need to CONNECT with you and greet you with all four paws on the floor. This releases you from constantly telling your dog to stay off and very effectively teaches an important life skill of greeting humans with four paws on the floor. It also meets their need to say 'Hello to the humans they love.'

Puzzle Pieces for Success

Piece 1: Be consistent. Teach everyone who greets your dog how to meet them when their paws on the floor.

Piece 2: Be prepared to greet your pup the **moment** you walk through the door, not after you put the groceries down.

Piece 3: If you physically cannot bend down, place a chair near the door allowing you to get closer to your dog without him jumping up.

Putting the Pieces Together

Step 1: Squat down and meet them at their level.

Step 2: Touch the dog with both of your hands on either side of their body.

Step 3: Take a couple of deep relaxing breaths as you slowly stroke them.

Step 4: Keep stroking and talking quiet until their wiggly body settles. When you feel them relax, keep stroking a little while longer.

Step 5: Teach your friends and family this method and your pup will soon keep their paws on the floor expecting the humans to come to them.

REMEMBER: Slow strokes and low voice will encourage calm and quiet. Quick strokes and high-pitched voice will energize them.

PIPER: SEARCHES OUT OF BOUNDS

In my many years as a K9 handler, Piper and I completed many searches while training with the Oklahoma City Firefighter USAR team. We both learned so much from them.

On one occasion Piper and I were preparing for an assessment to certify and become a deployable resource. The firefighters set up a double blind search for us, which meant I did not know where the 'search subject' was hidden.

Training without any knowledge of the location of the person buried under the rubble simulates real life and better prepares you to pay attention to your dog's body language and helps prevent unintentional cueing your dog.

The scenario for the search and the boundaries for Piper to stay within were communicated to me and we were given the signal to go. Now it was up the Piper to find her subject.

I said, "Search" and released her to do her job. Piper and I began our work of 'clearing the pile' which is what it's called when the dog moves across the rubble pile and does not alert, telling the handler there is nobody buried.

All of a sudden Piper sped off to the opposite end of the rubble. I knew she had located 'live human scent' by the way she was running directly to her target.

I told the firefighter climbing the rubble with us, "She's got him."

The firefighter replied, "Piper is heading out of bounds. There is nobody hidden that far." After further questioning and against my better judgment, I blew my whistle recalling Piper to me.

Piper completely ignored me. She didn't even look back to acknowledge the whistle. When she ignored me, I did not attempt to call her again, because at that point I knew she smelled 'live, human scent' and would not stop or turn around until she reached the person buried under the rubble.

The firefighter chuckled and said, "She's about to scare a homeless person, because none of the guys went that far." Just as he finished his sentence, Piper barked, indicating that she found her person.

I acknowledged Piper's alert, yelling as loud as I could, "My dog is alerting on Live Human Scent!" and the hidden firefighter vigorously rewarded her for her successful search.

We never figured out how or why the boundaries that day were much farther than originally planned. But what I did learn that day was to TRUST Piper and all of the hours we spent together finding people lost or buried under the rubble.

Over time your CONNECTION and trust in one another will go both ways. They put their faith and trust in you, and you get to return the favor by putting your trust and faith in them.

CONNECTION THROUGH BODY LANGUAGE

One of the easiest ways to support your Connection is by learning to become fluent in your dog's BODY LANGUAGE.

Dogs do not have words to communicate their needs, but they communicate with us on a continual basis through physical postures, nuance and body language. We are well served to begin to recognize this physical language, so we can more easily meet their needs and deepen the unspoken level of interaction that is so crucial to our canine/human partnership.

SIGNS OF STRESS

- Panting (short and quick)
- Yawning
- Licking their lips
- Refusing treats or grabbing them rudely
- Salivating profusely
- Abundant shedding
- Whites of eyes are visible
- Making themselves bigger/hackles raised: indicates fear
- Making themselves smaller: indicates they are terrified

SIGNS OF AGGRESSION
- Turns head away or turns body away
- Moves away (When a dog is on a leash, may attempt to

move behind you)
- Creeps, ears back
- Stands, crouches, tail tucked under
- Stiffens
- Stares
- Growls
- Snaps or bites

SIGNS OF EASE/PLEASURE

- Wiggly body
- Soft, relaxed body
- Lying down quietly
- Taking treats from you
- Turning over offering belly for a rub
- Easily responds to handler
- Free and easy movement
- Curving their body, saying, "Hey, I want to be your friend."
- Play bowing

APPROPRIATE DOG PLAY

- Role reversals: each taking in turn being on the bottom
- Soft, wiggly body language
- Taking breaks
- Drinking water
- Shaking it off
- Sniffing

TIP: If you are missing some or all of the above when dogs are playing, it's time to intervene!

REFINING THE COMMUNICATION

Some signs of stress are okay and can help our dogs grow confidence to navigate the world in which they live.

Many times, when I'm in a new environment, usually a store with a service puppy in training, I notice some panting, yawning and other 'stress' signals. At that point I connect with them by laying my hand on them, offering them a treat, taking a deep breath, and staying calm while allowing them time to assimilate their environment. Sometimes that's all it takes to diffuse the stress and we can move on.

If the stress becomes too much or increases and is not easily dissolved, I immediately remove them from the situation that is making them uncomfortable. I want to let them know 'all is well' and provide them with the relief they need to be quiet and comfortable.

When you offer support during times of stress without allowing it to become a big deal, you build trust. When you return to the same place that caused the stress before, they'll navigate it like a pro, because they learned it wasn't a big deal and you supported them through that learning process. This builds TRUST!

PRACTICE: CHECK IN

Life skill: Checking in is when the dog chooses to come back or look at you. This can be either on or off leash and develops as the connection with your pup grows. Checking in with their human is a behavior that appears naturally when the bond is strong.

Puzzle Pieces for Success

Piece 1: Notice when your dog looks in your direction.

Piece 2: Acknowledge them and immediately release them to continue their previous activities anytime they choose to 'Check in.'

Piece 3: Never scold your dog when they check in with you. (This can be difficult when they just finished chewing the shoestrings out of your shoes.)

Supplies: Treats, toys and an incredibly engaged, paying attention human.

Putting the Pieces Together

Step 1: Catch the moment your dog naturally checks in with you during the day.

Step 2: Acknowledge it with kind words, treats, or a quick game of tug.

Step 3: When your dog comes back while off leash playing, acknowledge them with attention, treats or an excited party.

Step 4: Immediately release them and give them permission to continue playing. This promotes 'Checking in' and returning to you and is a building block for awesome recalls!

TIP: If you take the opportunity to leash them up and 'kill' their fun when they choose to check in or come back, before long they will stop checking in with you – The practice of 'Checking in' is an ongoing interaction between you and your pup that develops over time and strengthens with practice. Continue to acknowledge your dog when they choose to look at you or return to you and notice over the next few weeks the difference in the frequency of 'Check In's.'

Behaviors that are encouraged will be repeated and become life skills.

PRACTICE: LOOK AT ME!

Life skill: 'Look at me' is the ability to request your dog's attention so they completely focus on you and wait for your next cue. It is skill that is useful in stressful situations to help manage the environment. And it is a skill that is useful in competition or detection when you need to give the dog another cue.

Puzzle pieces for Success

Piece 1: Keep teaching sessions very short.

Piece 2: Maximum of 3–5 repetitions.

Piece 3: Initially, practice only at home in a quiet environment.

Supplies: A dog on a leash, human and treats.

Beginning level: On leash

Step 1: Take a treat and hold it between your eyes.

Step 2: When your dog gazes toward the treat (your eyes) say, "Look."

Step 3: Move the treat from your eyes to their mouth.

Step 4: Repeat a couple of times.

Intermediate level: Off leash
You are ready to move onto the intermediate level when you say "Look" and your dog immediately looks into your eyes.

Step 1: When your dog is quiet, but not paying attention to you, surprise them, say "Look!"

Step 2: Bring the treat from your eyes to their mouth.

> **TIP:** Keep practicing in a variety of environments, but only a couple of times during each session. Try to surprise them and notice the speed at which they look into your eyes.

Mastery Level
You are only ready for the mastery level when your dog focuses on you when you practice inside the house, outside your home, on your daily walks and in ALL familiar environments.

Step 1: Take your dog to an environment that is distracting to him. Perhaps near a dog park, children's playground or busy shopping area.

Step 2: Say "Look." What happened? Did he gaze into your eyes?

Step 3: Give him a treat and make a huge deal about it. Give him several treats. Celebrate and acknowledge his response while telling him what a good dog he is.

TIP: At first, only practice once or twice in the most distracting environments. Be the best thing in your pup's life in this scenario. Bring their favorite tug toy and be prepared to engage with him.

Experiment with different surroundings with varying levels of distraction. If or when the distractions prove too much, be prepared to quickly add some distance between your pup and the distraction.

When I recognize that I have asked too much or moved too quickly with a pup, I know I need to modify the situation in some way. I use my excited voice, engage with the dog and do a bit of running around together. This serves as a 'Play Break' but what it really does is pulls their focus back toward me and away from the distractions.

TIP: Challenge your pup with particularly 'irresistible' situations and invite them through the practice to rise above the distractions and focus only on you. Progress slowly and move farther away when the distractions are too much. Then try again! Make it fun. Reward them vigorously when they do well!

THE POWER OF A STRONG FOUNDATION

Starting with CONNECTION gives you the framework and ultimate foundation that will help you build all of the independent skills you'll need as you move forward with your dog.

Connection naturally leads us to the other pieces of the puzzle of Meeting Your Dog's Needs and Regulating the Environment, because they are all integrated. It allows you to recognize what your dog needs in each moment and meet those needs especially when you encounter challenges along the way.

The additional power and beauty of the CONNECTION piece is that it is ALWAYS growing, expanding and becoming even more powerful in its capacity to support you and your dog in challenging situations.

It will serve you well as you begin to practice with the next pieces of the puzzle.

CHAPTER 3

MEETING YOUR DOG'S NEEDS

"Beneath every behavior is a feeling. And beneath every feeling, there is a need. When we meet that need rather than focus on the behavior, we begin to deal with the cause and not the symptom."

– Ashley Warner

I invite you to consider the next piece of the Puppy Puzzle, 'Meeting your Dog's Needs' as both a SCIENCE and an ART.

Every dog has basic needs, yet every dog is different. There are basic needs that every dog requires to survive. That's the SCIENCE part of the equation. But each dog is unique in personality, temperament and energy levels. Which is why each dog has different needs to help him thrive… that is the ART of it all.

The CONNECTION piece of the puzzle that we discovered in the previous chapter, will help you learn how to Meet Your Dog's Needs in a more individualized way. Meeting those needs will expand your dog's potential in their chosen jobs.

THE ART OF MEETING NEEDS

Meeting your dog's needs involves more than simply dumping food and water in their dish and turning them outside to use the bathroom and to entertain themselves.

Those are the most basic needs, and a dog will survive if he has those things. But in order for a dog to THRIVE, they need delicious, nutritious food and fresh water. They need Connection with their favorite human and time to be a dog. Dogs need exercise and predictable routines that include all kinds of canine enrichment and a safe, quiet place to rest.

Dogs need their humans to be reliable and dependable so they can grow in confidence in themselves and their abilities. They need an ally to protect them from 'scary' things and to advocate for their wellbeing. And they need a buddy to teach them how to navigate the interesting, sometimes crazy human world, while allowing them freedom to experience life in ways that encourage growth and confidence. In addition to keeping them safe and secure at the same time.

When your dog's needs are met on all levels, they begin to make more life affirming choices, they learn manners and life skills to navigate the world of people and make life easier for all.

I cannot overstate the positive impact you will see when you develop the habit of 'Meeting your Dog's Needs' before they are required to advocate for themselves. When this piece of the Puppy Puzzle is firmly in place, and your dog's needs are readily met, they will move from Surviving to Thriving and that is when the magic really starts to happen.

A CHANGE IN PERSPECTIVE

I once read a fascinating story about an elk in the Pocatello, Idaho zoo called Shooter. Shooter rescued a marmot that was drowning in his water tank. The elk noticed the little animal in crisis and lifted him out of his water tank and set it safely on the ground.

Shooter's keepers attributed this animal version of compassion to his 'lack of need.' Because all of his needs were abundantly met, Shooter was able to recognize another species in trouble and offer assistance to help meet the needs.

The educator at the zoo, Kate O'Connor said of Shooter's interesting behavior, "When the basic needs of a life form are being met, you start seeing more elaborate behaviors that engage their brains in different ways. Behaviors that would have been basically for survival, are now used in ways that are more complex and advanced."

With survival no longer an issue, meaning all of Shooter's meals arrived on a regular schedule, water was readily available and he was provided daily enrichment with plenty of space to exercise, his capacity to recognize when another species needed assistance and respond accordingly was elevated. With his own needs met, Shooter was able to think, comprehend and respond at a more advanced level of intelligence and awareness.

If an elk in a zoo can display this expanded level of awareness, connection and compassion, just imagine the potential of our dogs.

SURVIVE OR THRIVE

The power of 'Meeting our Dog's Needs' influences every cell of their biology. This crucial second puzzle piece, helps us move them into a position of THRIVING, which allows them to use greater levels of intelligence to succeed in life maximizing their potential in their chosen jobs.

Science has recognized that 'an organism is capable of only two modes of operation: growth or survival.' The systems involved in digestion, assimilation, respiration, nerve function and mental capacity and the chemical, hormonal and biological processes that accompany these processes are all influenced by this 'growth or survival' position.

When a body or system receives the impression from its environment that it is *safe*, that body will automatically shift into life-expanding, growth-based actions that allow all biological, mental and emotional systems to function at peak levels.

When the environment is perceived as *unsafe,* that same organism will shift into survival mode, and all those life-affirming actions like higher mental processes will cease, so the energy can be used by the organism to simply stay alive.

To put it simply, when a system is stressed, it is very inefficient. This reality is the same for humans as it is for dogs. If you can recall what it feels like in your mind and body when you're stressed and how limiting it feels to you… Understand that it feels the same way for your dogs.

When dogs are in a *'hard place'* they automatically move into survival and do not have the ability to learn new things or help others in difficult times. The biological response to stress moves them into an evolutionary pattern of system protection, which limits their ability to process information beyond the basics of 'fight or flight.'

If we want to be able to set them up for success to reach their maximum potential, we need to be aware of this important biological function and what we need to do to shift it.

LIFE CAN BE STRESSFUL

Dogs come into our lives from many different environments and situations. Even when we bring a dog home with the best of intentions, those first few days, WILL create STRESS in their system. In those moments, they are in a 'hard place.'

For a while the biology of your new dog will shift into survival as their surroundings move from known to unknown, expected to unexpected and familiar to unfamiliar. Time, awareness and consistency will be key to helping them move into Thriving in their current environment.

Puzzle piece – two: 'Meeting their Needs' becomes imperative at this time as your actions help them feel safe and secure enough to switch from the Survival mode generated by stress, into calm, comfort and security that will shift them into Thriving mode. This gives them the opportunity to change from Survival to Thriving.

Your job at this time is to:

- Provide connection with the new humans in their life.
- Protect their environment so they feel safe.
- Provide nutritious meals.
- Allow plenty of exploring and exercise in their new environment.
- Allow plenty of time to rest.
- Let them know that you are their advocate.

These important elements help your pup move quickly

through and out of the limits of surviving and into the growth of Thriving! When you meet your dog's needs on all levels, you increase their capacity to reach far beyond their training. Their potential accelerates just like Shooter the Elk, because they no longer have to advocate for their basic needs and they feel safe to try new things.

PRACTICE: TUG AND SETTLE

Life skill: Practice with this game gives your dog the ability to move from an excited energy into a calm one, in a very short amount of time. This empowers them to maintain connection and interaction with you, regardless of the environment around you, so you can move them through difficult situations with ease.

Puzzle Pieces for Success

Piece 1: Let the dog win.

Piece 2: Allow the dog to win before their energy escalates to frenzied.

Piece 3: Keep playing time brief, 1–3 minutes.

Supplies: A dog on a leash, favorite tug toy, and treats.

Putting the Pieces Together

Step 1: Play tug with your puppy briefly. Allow the dog to win.
  TIP: We want to encourage the pup to pull straight back rather than throwing their heads from side to side. Let go of the toy when the pup is pulling straight back on his haunches, which encourages him to pull straight back.

Step 2: Stop the play. Sit quietly. Breathe deeply and relax within your own body. Allow time for them to settle. Give them ZERO instructions!

Initially they will be very excited. Your job is to continue the stillness and breathe deeply, giving them the freedom to move around a little while remaining on leash, but doing so quietly.

Step 3: Take a couple of very deep breaths, exhaling with a sigh.

Step 4: When your pup responds to your relaxation and chooses to be still. (They can be standing, sitting or lying down) begin the game again – Play tug!

Step 5: Repeat the process 2 or 3 times.

Finish the game

After the last tugging session, when they choose the calm, give them a few treats, enjoy the calm with a great belly rub.

PIPER VS THE HATS

Piper learned her job quickly, and shortly before her second birthday, she passed her first disaster search assessment.

A few weeks after Piper's success, the weather in Oklahoma turned bitter cold. I am NOT a cold weather person and prefer to stay inside when the temperatures drop. I like to be comfortable, why in the world would I go outside if I didn't have to? I soon learned the answer to that question.

Not long into this self-imposed restriction of zero outside time, Piper started destroying John's caps. I thought perhaps John left them somewhere she could easily reach them. So, my most reasonable solution was to put them away, where she couldn't get them. Problem solved... or so I thought.

The cold weather persisted, and I continued to stay inside with Piper, letting her out long enough throughout the day to take care of business, but not much else. And with the freezing temperatures too much for my warmth loving bones, I certainly allowed her no time to actually sniff, walk around or play.

*The next day I discovered **my** favorite search cap destroyed and the day after that I found her with my beach hat. She was about to turn it into her new favorite chew toy.*

*Now I knew something was up. None of **my** hats had been conveniently laying around for easy access. She figured out a way to get them, because I had not met her needs. She was bored, and the hats, even if they were on a shelf five feet high, became her favorite target.*

The cold weather had given me an 'excuse' for not meeting Piper's needs for exercise, sniffing, digging, chewing and interaction. My desire to be comfortable seemed reasonable to me, but it was unreasonable for Piper. The result: she discovered a way to meet her own needs... at the expense of our hats.

Lesson learned. Score: Piper – 4. Hats – 0.

IF YOU DON'T DO IT… THEY WILL

If we don't meet our dogs' NEEDS, they WILL find a way to advocate for themselves and it usually is not something we want them to do. When they are required to meet their own needs, because we haven't provided it for them, they will shift into stress mode and in an attempt to 'balance their own system.' They can and will adopt destructive behaviors to do it.

If you've ever seen a dog that lives on the street, who had to struggle for even the most basic of needs, you can see the survival stress in that animal. When they are in that sort of life position, they are often unpredictable, flighty and dangerous. They will do whatever it takes to meet their own needs.

When we bring dogs into our homes, either as young puppies or as more mature animals, we want to be sure they don't have to either advocate for themselves or meet their own needs, especially in the beginning. The needs of dogs aren't complex or complicated. They are basic, but vital for thriving.

In order to establish and support our dogs as they learn how to best navigate the human world, we need to provide them with nutrient rich food, fresh water, shelter and security. We also need to provide them with exercise, social interaction, mental engagement, and the freedom to make choices.

We need to provide them the time and space to do 'dog stuff,' running, sniffing and chewing. And even provide them with the freedom to do the annoying stuff like digging in the yard and chasing things that run.

Our dogs need unconditional love from their reliable people, predictable routines and a quiet place to rest. We are the source of these needs and when we consistently and regularly provide these simple yet powerful basics, our dogs naturally and effortlessly begin to thrive.

The following Practice is a wonderful way of Meeting your Dog's Needs in a way that is fun and playful while developing your growing connection.

PRACTICE: DISCOVERY WALK

Life skill: Discovery Walks are an excellent daily practice that combines ALL of the Puzzle Pieces. A great Discovery Walk encourages Connection through providing your pup with something he loves while Meeting their Need to safely explore their surroundings. You will notice many positive benefits when you take your dog on a Discovery Walk on a regular basis.

Puzzle Pieces for Success

Piece 1: Be willing to go at your dog's pace. This is his walk, not yours.

Piece 2: Be silent, be a statue when your dog pulls.

Piece 3: Remember: your actions affect your dog's responses. Allow freedom to explore, but do not allow pulling.

Supplies: A dog on a long leash (10–15 ft or shorter if needed for safety in your environment). Treats and a human ready to walk at the dog's pace while the dog sniffs or freeze when they pull.

Putting the Pieces Together

Step 1: Take your dog for a walk allowing them to lead.

Step 2: Pair the words "Go sniff" or "Follow your nose" with the action of the dog's nose moving toward the ground. (This connects the words to the action.)

Step 3: When your dog gets near the end of the leash say "Easy" giving them a signal they are almost at the end of their leash and need to slow down.

Step 4: As soon as they reach the end of the leash and keep pulling, STOP. FREEZE. Do NOT move or talk. ZERO interaction and ZERO eye contact here is the key to success. IGNORE them.

Step 5: Continue standing still until the dog moves toward you allowing slack in the leash.
   TIP: They do NOT have to return all the way to you. A small J in the leash is enough to keep moving.

Step 6: As soon as the dog moves allowing slack in the leash, say 'Let's go' and continue your walk. This forward movement is their reward for keeping slack in the leash and not pulling. They figure it out very quickly.

Step 7: Anytime and every time your dog looks back or comes all the way back to you, they are 'checking in' acknowledge them with touches, treats and kind words.
   TIP: Dispense treats down the seam of your pants on the side you want them for loose leash walking. Dogs will hang out where they receive the most goodies.

THE GIFT IS RETURNED TO US

The process of 'Meeting your Dogs Needs' can be one of the most rewarding pieces of the Puppy Puzzle. When you become fluent in speaking the language of 'Meeting your Dogs Needs' before they have to advocate for themselves, training is seamless, fun and the communication between you and your dog becomes something truly amazing.

Think of how you feel and how you function when your needs are met. Your dog feels the same way. The only difference is, he depends on YOU to help him arrive at that outcome. But it doesn't end there.

This Puzzle Piece is truly a GIFT we give to our canine companions. Remember how Shooter the elk was positively impacted by his nurturing environment and was able to extend his intelligence and service in such an amazing way to a fellow being in trouble. This life affirming scenario operates the same way for our dogs. In this case, the gift of this puzzle piece we provide, becomes a gift that will be returned to us time and time again.

CHAPTER 4

REGULATING YOUR DOGS ENVIRONMENT

"Like a plant that depends upon the environment to thrive, so does a dog."

– Sharon Dilley

We have discussed the first two Puzzle Pieces, **Connection** and **Meeting needs** and provided you with some 'Practices' to begin incorporating into your dog's everyday life. You probably have already noticed some positive differences in your training and everyday life with your little buddy.

The third and final piece of the Puppy Puzzle is what I call: **Regulating the Environment.** This is an important training element where YOU set up the environment, and then capitalize on his great choices. The dog has a choice to make, but the choice you want him to make is the easy one, the one that gets him what HE wants, treats, play time outside time, interaction with you, etc. Your choice sets him up for success. Sort of like 'stacking the deck' in a game of cards, you know you're going to win, because you have set it up that way.

The impact Regulating the Environment has on the speed with which your pup learns how to navigate the human world is huge. When the dogs learn that their choices affect what happens to them, they learn very quickly without endless repetitions.

Regulating or managing the environment allows you to control the situation allowing you to support him in the beginning stages of learning and set the environment up for your dog to succeed. If there are too many distractions in the environment, it has the potential to overwhelm and possibly shift your dog into 'survival mode,' which ultimately limits their ability to process and maintain information.

This important third Puzzle Piece sets your dog up for learning success. When the dog experiences success/rewards immediately, they will repeat the behavior. This expands their comprehension of the tasks you outline for them and encourages learning as an astounding rate.

SETTING UP THE ENVIRONMENT FOR SUCCESS

Regulating the Environment simply means to begin the teaching and learning process in an environment that ensures a positive outcome for the pup. An environment that is narrow enough where the choice you ultimately want them to make is the easy one. And when the dog chooses the unfavorable outcome, you remain neutral and allow natural consequences to be the teacher. The environment may be your living room or backyard, or any location where your pup is not concerned about their surroundings. When you choose a quiet place free from distractions, your dog's attention will be on you and what you are asking them to do, rather than on any unknown variable that may be around them.

A regulated environment also includes YOU. When working with your dog, maintain a position of neutral emotion so your dog can make errors without drama or scolding. You simply let natural consequences be the teacher. Remaining neutral will allow your dog to respond to instructions with greater confidence and learn as a faster pace.

This place of neutrality gives us access to better communication with our dogs. It sets us up so we can remain neutral when they make a choice that isn't appropriate and helps us remain focused when things are going well, allowing us to respond rather than react to their less than ideal choices. It becomes a matter of the dog makes a choice and then it's my turn to make a choice.

Regulating the Environment expands your dog's ability to

learn, increasing their potential in their chosen jobs. When we are prepared to adjust the outside influences, we are setting a tone that includes every piece of the Puppy Puzzle. At this stage of our practice, every piece of the puzzle is activated, which allows for greater levels of success.

EXAMPLES TO REGULATE THE ENVIRONMENT

When you regulate the environment, you set up each situation so the dog chooses the thing you ultimately want as well. Below are a few examples to regulate the environment to ensure successful outcome. Let these suggestions get you started and be creative in applying them to your surroundings.

Here are a few ideas to get your creative mind going:

- Put your dog on a leash if you are not 100% sure he will come when you call.
- Keep your dog tethered to you in the house until he learns to use the bathroom outside rather than inside.
- Allow him rest/sleep in his kennel when you are gone so he can't get into trouble while you're away.
- Move to the opposite side of the street when there is a scary, barking dog approaching you or behind a fence.
- Use baby gates to keep him closer to you in your home, but still allow freedom.
- Keep him on long line when outside teaching a new job related skill.

The possibilities are endless and each time you manage the environment and create more opportunities for your dog to choose, he develops more confidence in his own ability to navigate the human world. As his knowledge of making great choices expands and he develops the skills to successfully navigate the human world, you will relax this piece of the Puppy Puzzle. His ability to manage life's challenges, becomes simple and automatic.

PIPER: THE 5 MINUTE FAILURE

There are many different components to the FEMA equivalent assessment that allows a dog to be a part of a search and rescue team, ready for deployment to search for the missing and buried under the rubble.

One of those assessments is a five minute Down / Stay, where the dog is lined up with several other dogs while the handlers move out of sight. The test requirement states that a dog can move no more than a body length from where the handler places them.

In my training work with Piper, we were successful in establishing a strong and consistent 'lie down.' But with less than a month before our scheduled assessments, she failed a mock test when she did not remain where I left her. She got the 'down' part correct and she remained on her belly, but the 'stay' part wasn't solid and she creeped forward, more than the allowed body length.

This belly scoot would not pass the search and rescue test. I had to find a way to help her truly understand that 'stay' meant to remain exactly where I left her. She wasn't allowed to let the activity of the environment overrule her direction to stay where I placed her.

My approach was to start the entire 'down/stay' protocol from the beginning and build a process that gave Piper a choice and capitalized on her choice. I wanted to be able to set her up in such a way that she could CHOOSE her behavior in any environment and be rewarded for it, instead of me making that choice for her.

I attached a leash to her collar and was fully prepared to stand in my living room (a very boring environment) all day long if that is what it took for her to choose to lay down and relax. She soon grew tired of standing and laid down. The moment she moved to her belly, I placed treats between her front paws and quietly said, "Lay down." Piper figured out very quickly when she laid down, she was abundantly rewarded, but when she stood up, she received nothing.

As soon as she became proficient at choosing to relax and lie down in the living room, we moved outside and practiced there. When she became consistent outside, we moved to a public, but not very busy shopping market. When that worked well, we moved to a park where there were people, dogs, other critters and activity everywhere. I started small and progressed slowly.

Piper built her confidence at each level and recognized the power of her 'choices' to develop greater consistency in more challenging environments.

By starting in a boring environment with little to no distraction, and increasing the stimulation incrementally in each new situation, I gave Piper the opportunity to recognize her own success at each level. In a very short amount of time this level of confidence allowed her successfully perform her 'down/stay' in any environment, including the chaotic and stressful assessment environment.

Piper's better understanding of what I needed from her gave her the confidence and provided her with the ability to pass our search and rescue test the following month. When I placed her in a Down/Stay, she remained exactly where I left her and never moved a muscle.

*** The PRACTICE: I used to teach the Down/Stay is outlined in the following Chapter. I highly encourage you to teach Calm as a Default Behavior below before beginning the Emergency Down/Stay. When you begin giving the command to lie down before the dogs develop Calm as a Default behavior, you will be forever using the command rather than allowing your dog to learn to settle themselves in a variety of environments.

SETTING UP SUCCESS

We want our dogs to be happy, vibrant and thoughtful creatures. This capacity to encourage and expect our dogs to use their natural intelligence sets them up to perform their jobs with greater understanding and increases their ability to be independent thinkers.

Regulating the Environment helps us support our dogs as they develop any new skill or as they refine an already existing one. The power of deliberately creating an environment that sets the dog up for success in the beginning helps grow the dog's confidence. They learn the simple things and then are able to generalize the learning to other more difficult situations.

MANAGING TIME AND EXPECTATIONS

It's important to realize that working with our dogs isn't always a linear process. Being flexible is important when the unexpected happens. Sometimes you have to make quick adjustments in the middle of a lesson to ensure success. If something goes differently than originally planned, (which is common) stop the training process immediately, decide what is needed to communicate more clearly the training goals and make adjustments ensure a successful outcome.

The dog's ability to absorb information and learn new skills will increase dramatically as they continue to encounter success when the environment is as distraction free as possible. The success they experience becomes hardwired in their brain and body as they realize that their choices affect their lives.

As the surroundings change, and the distractions and difficulty increases, your pup already has a memory of success and how to achieve what they want. It then becomes easy for him to make good choices at more challenging levels when distractions increase.

As their skill and proficiency advances, it's time to change environments. Shift your location to a quiet park or move from inside your home to outside your home. Be conscious of how quickly you move to new surroundings based on how comfortable your pup is in each new situation.

If they are comfortable and continue making the choices you desire, keep practicing. If you notice signs of stress, panting, yawning, no longer taking treats, move back to the more comfortable environments. Learning a new skill takes a tremendous amount of energy and focus. As your pup becomes more proficient at a skill, they will generalize it to different situations and any location.

PRACTICE: CALM AS A DEFAULT BEHAVIOR

Three Different Methods = One calm dog!
1. Off leash
2. On leash
3. While dining

Life skill: Calm As a Default Behavior teaches the dog to remain calm in a variety of situations. His calm demeanor becomes the go to even in stressful situations and becomes an automatic life skill. It fosters the ability within the dog to be at ease and settled in any situation. A calm, confident 'working dog' is better able to think and complete his job than a dog who lives in a more excited state. For pet and service dogs, the ability to relax while moving through a variety of environments is an invaluable skill. When you promote this skill, the dog automatically goes to their place of quiet in virtually any situation.

PROMOTING THE CALM OFF LEASH

Puzzle Pieces for Success

Piece 1: Begin in an environment with very few distractions.

Piece 2: Remain neutral and silent.

Piece 3: Surprise your dog by randomly dropping treats when they are calm.

Supplies: Bowls of strategically placed treats around your home, a dog moving through their day and a human who is paying attention.

Putting the Pieces Together: Off leash

Step 1: Watch for a time when your pup lies down and is NOT focused on you. A time when they are simply relaxing.

Step 2: Silently go to them and drop a few treats between their paws on the floor.
   TIP: If your dog stands up before you put the treat on the floor, put the treat back in the bowl or treat pouch and move on. Remain neutral, your dog did nothing wrong, do not scold them. The less interaction here, the better.

Step 3: Move on with your daily life, always on the lookout for your pup to lie down without focusing on you. The goal is to catch your dog CHOOSING calm behavior.

Step 4: When you see the behavior again, capture it by placing treats between their paws on the floor.

Step 5: Practice 1–4 as often as possible inside your home.

Step 6: Practice outside.

Step 7: Practice Everywhere.

TIP: Catching the behavior for the first time takes the most stealth. After the first time, the dog learns very quickly that when you walk toward them, their job remain is in place.

Promoting The Calm: On leash

Capture the Calm: On leash

Puzzle Pieces for Success

Pieces 1: Allow enough slack in the leash for your dog to sit, stand or lie quietly.

Piece 2: Take a deep breath and let it out with a sigh.

Piece 3: Stand quietly. The first few times this is an exercise in patience on your part.

Supplies: A pocket or treat pouch full of treats. A dog on leash and a human willing to do nothing and say nothing.

Putting the Pieces Together

Step 1: Walk with your dog on leash in a familiar area, stop and stand quietly. This takes patience the first time. Remain quiet and do not engage with your dog.

Step 2: When the dog chooses to lie down, place a treat on the ground between their paws.

Step 3: Say, "Let's go" and continue your walk.

Step 4: Repeat steps 1–3 multiple times throughout your walk, always releasing them from the chosen calm quickly before they move on their own saying, "Let's Go!"

TIP: Do NOT give cues or instructions to the pup at this time. Allow your actions to be their guide. Dogs read body language very well and will respond accordingly. They will learn this skill very quickly.

Step 5: Practice in as many different environments as possible.

Promoting The Calm: While Dinning
Capture the Calm: While Dining

Puzzle Pieces for Success

Piece 1: Focus on your dog 100% in the beginning. Do NOT eat a meal.

Piece 2: Allow enough leash for the dog to sit, stand or lie down.

Piece 3: Find your patience and be prepared to sit and wait them out silently.

Supplies: Treats within easy reach, a dog on a leash and a table for the human to sit. I like to have a cup of tea while I wait them out the first time.

Putting the Pieces Together

Step 1: With your dog on a leash, sit at the table.

Step 2: Do not interact with your dog. Read a book or drink a beverage.

Step 3: When he/she lies down, silently place a treat between their paws.

Step 4: Continue placing treats between their paws at frequent intervals the first time.

Step 5: Keep the first time short (about five minutes), release the dog with a "Let's go" and move away from the table.
    TIP: The goal is for the dog to remain in place until you say, "Let's go."

Step 6: Take a Play Break. Have FUN! Thinking is hard work for them!

    TIP: The location your dog chooses to lie down in the beginning isn't important. What is important is the dog choosing the behavior, choosing to be calm and lie down on his own without your *guidance, luring, or instruction.* Be sure to acknowledge the smallest and first attempts of the desired behavior. If the dog jumps up before you place the treat between their paws, do NOT give the treat!
    Over time you'll have a dog that chooses Calm As a Default

Behavior and an automatic life skill!

ONE CALM DOG: ANYTIME, ANYWHERE
Capture the Calm: In Public

Puzzle Pieces for Success

Piece 1: Focus on your dog 100% of the time.

Piece 2: Find a quiet store that allows pets.

Piece 3: Do NOT attempt to shop in the beginning. 100% Focus on your dog.

Putting the Pieces Together

It's time to take your dog public when he lies down quickly off leash, on leash and at the dining room table in your home. Once a dog figures out that when you stop, they lie down and receive a treat, they generalize very quickly.

Step 1: Take your pup to a boring store where they allow pets.

Step 2: Go on a Discovery Walk inside the store.

Step 3: Stop and hold the leash where your dog can stand, sit or lie down without the leash pulling, but no more. Stop and look at the shelf in front of you. Do NOT make any attempt to get your dog to lay down.

Step 4: Wait them out. Zero interactions.

Step 5: The second the dog lays down, place a few treats on the floor between your dog's paws. The first time is usually easier than when you started in your home, because the dog already knows exactly what is going to happen if they lie down and remain in place. The only thing you have changed is their surroundings.

Step 7: Take a Play Break! They have worked hard.

TIP: Again, if they stand up before you place the treats on the floor, simply put them back in your pocket and continue waiting for them to CHOOSE to lie down.

Mastery level
Your dog is ready for this level when he demonstrates proficiency at ALL previous levels.

Step 1: Walk behind a shopping cart, stop, and when they lie down, place treats between their front paws.

Step 2: Stop at a counter (in a store that is not busy) to 'check out.' Wait for them to settle and place treats between their paws when they lie down. (I let the employees at the store know what I am doing and they usually love to assist in the teaching process.)

Step 3: Practice in variety of situations. Pay attention when your pup is not comfortable enough to lie down. Leave and try it again another day.

TIP: The speed of progression is dependent upon the dog. Some dogs soar through Mastery level and generalize very quickly, and others take more time. Move forward at your dog's pace.

One Final Note: Once your pup masters the Calm in many environments, when they choose NOT to lie down, it tells you that they aren't comfortable enough in their current environment to be calm and quiet. This is communication. Figure out what is bothering them and correct it. The same is true when the pup is calm and quiet in his kennel and all of the sudden they begin to whine or bark. At that point, they may be saying, "I have diarrhea or I have to pee so bad I cannot contain it."

When you are well versed in your dog's body language, you understand the communication more quickly and have the ability to respond which further encourages your Connection with your pup.

MANAGING ENVIRONMENTS AND POSITIVE ASSOCIATIONS

Part of the mastery of Regulating the Environment comes from our ability to be prepared, let go of mistakes and plan ahead to prevent those mistakes from happening again. Our goal is to manage our dog's surroundings, so they learn to associate the things that might normally make them uncomfortable, with something positive, thus encouraging their confidence and growth.

All is not lost when you encounter challenging times as long as you maintain your Connection and Meet the Needs of your dog.

Stress does not always come from the environment, sometimes a dog is simply more timid and afraid of life. Those dogs need to be allowed to move forward at their own pace and Regulating the Environment will help them do that with greater ease.

PIPER: MAYHEM AT THE DOG PARK

When Piper was six months old, I took her to a dog park to play and socialize with other dogs. (I am now very careful if I take my dogs to dog parks!)

On this particular day, there was a large boxer at the park as well. He approached Piper and before I could get to her, he had her pinned to the ground. I told the owner to get her dog off

Piper and she complied. As we were walking away, the dog repeated the behavior again. Once more I told the owner to control her dog and we headed toward the exit. Before I could get to the outside gate, the boxer came toward Piper a third time.

But this time Piper was having none of it. Piper lunged at the other dog growling and snarling like a savage. She pinned the boxer who outweighed her by at least twenty pounds to the ground so fast that I did not have time to react. She clearly said, "NO MORE!" The boxer's owner was shocked and said, "That's the first dog that has ever pinned him. It's probably a good lesson for him."

While it may have been a good lesson for that dog, it wasn't one that was beneficial for Piper.

I noticed after this incident every time she saw another dog, she immediately began to growl, it was barely audible, but it was a clear sign that she was never going to allow herself to be in that position again. An aggressive dog does not make a good search and rescue dog.

Growling at other dogs is a problem for a search and rescue canine who needs to get along with other animals when on deployment. Piper growling at other dogs could have ended her search career before it ever started.

POSITIVE ASSOCIATIONS ARE IMPORTANT

Positive social interactions are paramount for young puppies and dogs who benefit from being out in the world becoming accustomed to new and different surroundings. If the pup perceives the social interaction as negative rather than positive, the attempt at socialization is self-defeating and as in Piper's case, can be catastrophic.

When teaching a pup to be comfortable in their surroundings, move slowly and be certain that PUZZLE PIECE 3: Regulating the Environment is FIRMLY IN PLACE. As your awareness of this piece becomes more refined, you'll begin to recognize in an instant if the surroundings are beneficial or not and what you can do immediately to change them.

Take your time, be aware, notice what you notice and respond accordingly. Don't force, don't rush and always CONNECT with your dog. They'll tell you with their body language if they're feeling secure enough to learn and work, or if they're feeling threatened or afraid and need to leave the situation.

Notice your pup's body language. What are they telling you?

TAKE THE SCARY AWAY

If you find yourself in a situation or environment that creates anxiety or fear in your dog, YOU are the key to converting it into a positive association. You have the power to 'take the scary away' when you reassure them in the moment through kind words, gentle stroking and giving treats or by creating distance from the 'scary thing.' This gives your pup the time and space to figure out that they are safe, and that you will take care of them when they are feeling less than confident.

The important component of this 'Practice' comes when you pair something your pup enjoys with the 'scary' or new situation. CONNECT with kind words, touch, give them treats or play with them to communicate, 'All is well, and I will help you through this.'

Each time something wonderful happens when your dog is fearful or shy, you share a little of your confidence and increase their ability to better handle stressful situations in the future.

If you notice signs of stress or fear in your dog, be sure to manage your own stress levels as well. Pay attention to yourself and take a few deep, calming breaths. When you allow yourself to settle, you create an opportunity for your dog to follow your lead and to settle as well.

If his body language continues to communicate that their stress level is increasing instead of decreasing, move away and create more distance from the situation. As your dog's comfort increases, move closer to the 'scary,' allowing your dog to set the pace.

Be prepared to leave any environment if your dog does not settle in a short amount of time. It is better to stop the training session and try again another day than it is to push through and possibly create more issues. Many times, when you leave a situation and try it again the next day, the dog is ready to meet the challenge. Sometimes all they need is time and reassurance that you are supporting them.

PRACTICE: NAVIGATING THE WORLD

Life skill: This practice will help you recognize that you and your pup can successfully navigate any situation. When you encounter a stressful circumstance and you notice you pup growing scared or fearful, I invite you to apply the steps below to teach them that life is good and that you will support them through the 'scary.'

When you face challenging situations and you make spectacular errors in judgment as I did when I took Piper to the dog park, the ability to work through them quickly is vital for the dog's well-being.

Puzzle Pieces for Success

Piece 1: Notice your dog's body language. What are they telling you? Is their tail wagging? Stiff? Tucked? Are they leaning against you or hiding behind you? Backing up and ready to bolt? Are they tense all over? Are the trembling? Or are they tentatively moving forward? Telling you they are a little scared but want to investigate. Allow them to set the pace?

Piece 2: Allow processing time. Don't force or attempt to rush them through it.

Piece 3: Bring treats and toys EVERY TIME YOU LEAVE THE HOUSE!

Supplies: A dog on a leash, high value treats, a favorite toy and a patient human.

Putting the Pieces Together

Step 1: When you are in a situation that is scary, difficult or new, allow time for the dog to process their surroundings. Take a couple of deep calming breaths and allow them to have a little time to assimilate the environment.

TIP: The first time I take service puppies in training to the grocery store, I stop inside the door and allow them as much time as needed to process the new smells and activity. Sometimes I take them on a quick stroll through the store and other times we leave going no further depending on the puppy's comfort level. Observing your dog in these situations will make it easy for you to determine the best course of action in that moment.

Step 2: Pair something your dog enjoys (touches, kind words, treats or toys) with the source of the scary or new situation.

For Piper, each time we met another dog, I brought out her frisbee and we played a quick game of tug. This provided a distraction and paired the 'scary' (meeting another dog) with her favorite pastime, tugging. Over time, when she spotted another dog, she chose to look at me for a positive experience.

Piper grew to be incredible with other dogs, very kind and gentle and is now my best puppy trainer.

Step 3: Create more distance from the source of the 'scary.' Taking a few steps away is sometimes all it takes to increase their comfort level. Allow the dog to set the pace moving forward.

Step 4: Be willing to leave if your dog's stress signals increase or do not decrease in a short amount of time. Some days it's simply time to stop, relieve the pressure and allow everyone in the situation to calm down.

PIPER: SEARCHING – FROM 8 WEEKS TO MASTERY

I started teaching Piper the elements of the 'search game' as soon as we brought her home at eight weeks old. I very carefully regulated her environment from day one.

*In the beginning, I supported her through Connection, with lots of kind words and touch. I met her needs by providing all of the things a puppy could possibly desire. And I Regulated her Environment by setting up problems so simple that she succeeded **every single time.** Success came very easy in the beginning stages of learning. Life in these early days for Piper, was one gigantic party.*

Embedded in each game along the way were important elements of the search and rescue job she needed to learn: 1) Find the missing person. 2) Bark immediately. 3) Never leave the missing person until I arrived.

Piper's first 'search' was down a narrow hallway with my husband, John holding and squeaking her favorite toy duck. As she progressed, we added the next step where John moved around the corner out of Piper's view.

When I released her saying, "Search," she immediately ran around the corner to play tug with her prized toy and her favorite human. This simple yet meaningful game became the foundation of her search work and as her confidence grew, I set up more difficult scenarios.

As Piper progressed, when she ran around the same corner to locate John, he was not visible. Immediately, her nose went to the ground and engaged her sense of smell. She figured out in that moment how to use her nose to find her 'missing human.' Each time she found the human scent, she was abundantly rewarded with her favorite game, tugging until I arrived.

Every time I set up the environment to ensure her success, I implemented the components of finding, barking and remaining with the victim. Piper never had an opportunity to fail. We built the layers and processes of a successful search slowly, ensuring her 'win' each time. As she became more proficient at the easy games, I slowly increased the difficulty, again Regulating the Environment so Piper experienced success at each level.

When it came time to actually move to a pile of rubble to find a concealed subject, (an Oklahoma City Firefighter) Piper was able to complete her search with resounding success – and she did it at the tender age of only seven months old.

Piper has gone on to become a talented and respected search and rescue dog, who time and time again amazes me with her abilities. Most of the time knowing even more than the people around her. The foundations of success in the early days increased her confidence. Adding the fundamentals of finding the missing, barking and remaining with the person gave her the basic skills so when the challenging scenarios came, there was zero questions in her mind of what her job required.

Regulating the environment is a powerful teaching method and one I use frequently. In the following practice, you will be controlling the 'Environment, the resource' (going through the door) not the dog. When you shift your focus from controlling what the dog is doing, to 'controlling the resource' and Capture your dog's choice, learning happens at an astounding rate.

PRACTICE: WAIT AT THE DOOR

Life skill: 'Wait at the door' is a Practice that teaches your dog to remain in place when any door or gate opens. It also helps your dog make the connection between their choices and your responses. This simple practice teaches them how their behavior makes a difference in their world. It increases Connection, because they need to check in with you to gain permission and it Regulates the Environment until the dog learns self-control. *The following practice is a wonderful method to teach your pup how to remain in place when the human forgets to give the instruction to 'wait.'*

Puzzle Pieces for Success

Piece 1: Allow freedom for the dog to move.

Piece 2: *Control the resource, not the dog!* The resource is moving through the door.

Piece 3: Remain neutral and silent.

Supplies: A door and a dog on a leash, a human and a toy.

Putting the Puzzle Together

Beginning level

Step 1: Walk to the door with a dog on a loose leash and reach for the doorknob. If your pup is like most, they will jump and push forward to move through the door.

Step 2: Drop your hand to your side. Your pup will back up a little. Do not restrict your dog's movement, keep the leash loose allowing freedom to move around. The leash is only for safety, if the dog accidentally bolts through the door.

Step 3: Reach for the doorknob again. Your pup will again attempt to move forward. That's okay. Drop your hand to your side again.

Step 4: Repeat steps 1–3 as many times as it takes for your pup to remain in place or back up when you reach for the door.

Step 5: Once they remain in place, open the door a little bit more. Your dog will move forward again anticipating going through the door.

Step 6: Close the door. (*Move slowly and be careful. Do not close their nose in the door.*)

Step 7: Do not say anything at this point. No corrections or instructions. Allow the dog's choice to determine how much you open the door. His choice affects your response and vice versa.

Step 8: Open and close the door until your dog simply stays back and looks up to you. (The look on the dog's face at this point is priceless—One of what are you doing?) Body position is unimportant, they can be sitting or standing.

Step 9: When you can open the door almost enough to go through, say, "Let's Go!" and move through the door quickly.

Step 10: Take a play break!

   TIP: The first few times you play around with this, success needs to come easily and quickly!

Intermediate level

Before moving onto this level, establish the regular practice of your dog backing up, sitting or standing still as soon as your hand moves to open the door. Dogs learn this concept very quickly, because the resource they want is walking through the door and you have captured their decision, opened the door and given permission to go through.

Step 1: Practice the steps in the Beginning level with *every* door or gate you encounter.

Step 2: Use the same principle when opening the kennel for your dog to come out, teaching the dog to remain in place until you say, "Let's Go."

Mastery Level: Phase I – Connect the word 'WAIT'

When you and your pup have mastered walking nicely through virtually any door or gate without instructions and they automatically 'Wait' in place, it is time to connect the word 'WAIT' to the desired action.

TIP: Attach words to behaviors after the dog learns the desired behavior.

Step 1: Walk to the door, say "WAIT." Then open the door.

Step 2: Be ready to close the door if they decide to get a jump on you and move through it.

TIP: You have been silent while teaching to this point, allowing the pup to think and make a choice. Sometimes when you begin talking, they will respond to the sound of your voice rather than the words you are saying. Be prepared to close the door if they move when you say "WAIT."

Step 3: Say "Let's Go" and walk through.

TIP: Once the "WAIT" request is solid, you will be able to use it in other scenarios without the door. For example: when exiting a vehicle or when you need to step outside to pick up a package and your dog needs to stay in place for a short time, etc.

Mastery level: Phase II: Add Duration

When your pup clearly understands the word, 'WAIT,' you can begin to add more time before you give the cue, "Let's Go" and move to go through the door.

Step 1: Walk to the door, say "WAIT" then open the door

immediately.

Step 2: Count to 5 before giving the "Let's Go" instruction.

TIP: As with previous levels, ensure success before lengthening the time your dog remains in place after you open the door. You will reach your goal quicker if you progress slowly ensuring success at each level than moving too fast through the steps and having to go back and repeat them.

Finishing the Practice: End all practices when your dog experiences success. Go through the door, play, take a fun walk or just enjoy being outside.

BUILD ON SUCCESS

Regulating the Environment is the final foundational piece of The Puppy Puzzle. This important Puzzle piece helps you set up the environment so success is easily attained by your canine companion.

Regulating the environment to such a degree that your dog experiences success daily builds trust in the relationship and confidence in themselves. When you Set up the environment for success, the dogs learn how to make choices without fear of failure of scolding or punishment. And learning escalates at an astounding rate.

As you become more proficient at managing all three pieces of the Puppy Puzzle: **1. Connection 2. Meeting Needs and 3. Regulating the Environment**, your dog will be able to learn and grow in a way that gives them access to their maximum potential.

Because of the CONNECTION you created, they trust you.

Because you MEET THEIR NEEDS, they no longer have to advocate for themselves. And because their ENVIRONMENT IS REGULATED, they figure out that their choices make a difference in their lives.

When all of the Puzzle Pieces are practiced daily, your dog begins to understand that they have an ally in this human world and that their choices affect your responses. Now let's learn some techniques for implementing them into your daily life.

PART II

PUTTING THE PIECES TO WORK

CAPTURE, IGNORE,
INTERRUPT and REPLACE, or INTERRUPT AND RESET

Techniques in this section when implemented consistently alleviate much of the challenge of getting our dog to do what we want. CAPTURE makes the most of your dog's positive behaviors. IGNORE allows you to let go of the need for your dog to be a perfectly behaved. INTERRUPT, REPLACE, and RESET gives you a method of saying, "We're not going to do that, we're going to this instead."

These practices will help you respond to your pup's behaviors giving them valuable feedback quickly and effectively about the actions they are engaged in right now. Your responses tell your pup which behaviors are great and worthy of being repeated and which behaviors do not need repeated. Dogs want to please their favorite humans, many times it comes down to communication with your dog. Once they figure out what works for them, they are more than happy to do it!

CHAPTER 5

CAPTURE

"The brilliance of your future lies in the choices you make today."

– Susan Garrett, *DogsThat.com*

By now you may have noticed a pattern in how we encourage our dogs to move out of simply surviving into thriving. The consistent implementation and practice of the three foundational puzzle pieces of **Connection, Meeting Needs** and **Regulating the Environment** helps your dog learn very quickly while enjoying the process. Life becomes one big game and fun for all involved. This simple yet powerful structure helps you create the ultimate learning environment.

Now, let's learn how to capitalize on the many great behaviors you already witness in your dog.

CAPTURE BEHAVIORS YOU WANT TO SEE AGAIN!

Capturing is a method of acknowledging the behaviors you like which encourages your pup to repeat them. Remember, a behavior that is rewarded is a behavior that will be repeated. It's a method of saying, "YES," the action you are currently engaged in is exactly what is needed in this situation. "Capturing" a behavior tells the dog very clearly that what they are doing in this **present** moment is a great choice, one worthy of repeating. Basically, what you are getting proficient at, is 'catching them being good.'

When you recognize how powerful and simple the 'Capture' method is, you gain the ability to move through life noticing your dog's behaviors today and saying, "YES!" to the ones you want to see tomorrow.

Over time, this practice will become a repeating pattern of

your dog doing something good, you acknowledge it, and then repeating it all over again. **A behavior CAPTURED is a behavior repeated!** Even the behaviors you do NOT want.

SMOKY AND THE OUTSIDE CAFÉ

In my early days of training dogs, I had the opportunity to work with a lively pup named Smoky. He was a four-month old bundle of energy, and I was still a young trainer discovering what worked and what didn't.

I was attempting to follow the advice of a more experienced trainer who told me how to teach dogs to lie down under a table while eating. "Give the dog enough leash to sit or lie down and allow them to choose when they lie down. Then give him a treat on the ground immediately following their choice." We did our best to honor the instructions. Smoky had ideas of his own.

One day, my son Nick and I were puppy wrangling while eating lunch at an outdoor cafe. The problems started when Smoky chose to go around the chair leg, then under the table to sniff all the amazing smells. Nick moved that chair. No problem, Smoky just moved to the next one and wound himself around it. He then proceeded to the next chair and did the same thing, knocking it over.

This strategy clearly wasn't working, but I was determined to follow through with the instructions I had been given. Nick moved all the chairs so there was nothing left for Smoky to knock over or wind himself around and I shortened the leash. (We Regulated the Environment.)

Smoky was not having any part of laying down quietly under the table or anywhere for that matter. He was a little terror for the first thirty to forty-five minutes, and I was beginning to wonder if the advice I had been given was valid.

I continued with the instructions, "All pups will soon wear themselves out and lay down on their own. Keep quiet and be patient." Our meal arrived and Smoky suddenly laid down and completely relaxed on his own.

I placed some treats between his paws, saying nothing and continued dropping treats as we enjoyed our meal. By the time we were finishing the last bites of our hamburger, I ran out of treats. As a special reward I placed the final morsel of my hamburger between his paws and that sealed the deal.

As we stood up to leave, Smoky looked up at us as if to say, "You all go on, I'm staying right here." Life served him well under the table and Capturing his good behavior helped make it something he enjoyed doing from that day forward.

A TRIBUTE TO SMOKY

Smoky grew up to be an amazing drug detection dog and aided in getting many drugs off the streets of Oklahoma. He sadly lost his life in the line of duty doing what he loved with his partner. Thank you Smoky for your service and for all you taught me. I will forever remember my time with you.

ALL DAY, EVERYDAY

There are twenty-four hours in a day to notice your dog's amazing behaviors and Capture them. This reward system enables your pup to learn, their jobs, manners and life skills, providing them with the ability to navigate the human world with ease.

You don't need to wait until 'training time' to use this powerful strategy. As you move through the day doing 'regular things,' notice when your dog exhibits even the smallest action you want to see again and acknowledge the behavior in that moment. When you Capture even the smallest behavior, you can build it into the precise behavior you desire later.

Tell them, "Yes! That is exactly what I need in this moment!" Remember that any behavior acknowledged and rewarded (*CAPTURED*) is a behavior that will be repeated.

Think about the many different behaviors you witness each day that would be great manners or life skills. Each time you CAPTURE a behavior, the pup takes a mental snapshot of the action that created the acknowledgment and files it in its memory bank. *What you do with your dog today determines what his behavior is tomorrow*. Every time you tell your dog "Nice job" it ensures that they will repeat it in the future.

When your pup is not 'in training,' he is still learning. They are either learning what you want them to do or what you would prefer they not do. It's up to you and your responses.

If a pup doesn't choose what you desire this time, no problem. Set the situation up differently, change the Environment next time so you can achieve the desired result. Nothing is lost as the connection with you remains. Mistakes are simply feedback from them and opportunities for you to respond.

PRACTICE: SIMPLY CAPTURE

Life skill: Capture is a simple technique when applied correctly teaches the dog what you want them to do with very little effort. Learning comes quickly and naturally, because dogs are incredible at figuring out what works for them and repeating it. At the same time, they are figuring out what doesn't work for them and doing it less and less. It is another piece of the puzzle that builds Connection while Meeting the Needs of your dog as you carefully set up the Environment for success.

Puzzle Pieces for Success.

Piece 1: Gather a variety of healthy treats and place them for easy access around your home.

Piece 2: Be prepared to notice any behavior you want to see again tomorrow.

Piece 3: The action your dog is engaged in when you say, "YES!" and dole out the treat is the behavior he will remember. The behavior you 'Capture' is the one they will remember and repeat, even if it as a behavior you don't want.

Supplies: A dog, treats or tug toys, and a human ready to notice, acknowledge and CAPTURE the goodness!

Putting the Pieces Together

Step 1: Look for behaviors you like and want repeated.

Step 2: Acknowledge your pup with a "YES!" and communicate by giving treats or fun interaction with you.

>**NOTE:** If you do not have quick access to a treat or a toy, become the FUN! Get excited, run around or say, "Let's go get a treat!" And move quickly to distribute a treat. Your dog will pick up on your excitement and you still 'Captured' the moment you want repeated.

That's it! That is all there is to Capture! Simple yet powerful. Catch your pup being good. If you miss it, no problem simply CAPTURE it the next time. There will be countless moments for you to say, "YES!" to your pup.

CHARLIE: TREATS RAIN DOWN FROM THE SKY

When I first brought five-month old Charlie home, he didn't know the first thing about settling in the house and even less about laying down quietly while humans in the home shared a meal. If he wasn't barking, he was running circles around the living room and driving Piper crazy.

I'm not sure he even slowed down the first day. He was in a completely new environment. He'd had an eight hour car ride and was now sharing life with new people, cows, chickens, horses and smells he never encountered when he lived in the city. This life change had moved him into survival, he was in a 'tough place.'

In order to help him thrive in this new environment, I put the 3 pieces of The Puppy Puzzle to work. I Connected with him, Met his Needs and Regulated the Environment.

On the second day, Charlie still didn't lie down at my home, but he did lay down on a visit to my mother's house, when he hunkered down to chew on a water bottle. It wasn't exactly the desired behavior, but it was closer than running circles around my living room. So, I Captured it and dropped treats on the floor one right after another.

On the third day we made even more progress as Charlie laid down while I prepared dinner. Again, I surprised him by dropping treats on the floor between his front paws. At first, he jumped up to follow me as soon as he ate them, which isn't the final behavior I wanted. I ignored him when he jumped up.

My goal was to communicate to Charlie that when he quietly remained in place, treats come, but if he moved, treats go. The entire time I said not a word to him. When he stayed in place, I dropped treats between his front paws and continued cooking dinner. When he followed me, I ignored him.

On the fourth day at breakfast, Piper and Kali (the older dogs) were laying down while John and I shared a meal. Charlie sat, he received no treat. He continued sitting and stared at me. Still nothing. Not negative, but zero treats. Finally, he sighed and laid down. In the moment I dropped enough freeze-dried liver treats to make this moment one he remembered forever. This time he did not move when I walked away.

Score! He figured it out! Because I incorporated each piece of The Puppy Puzzle, Connection, Meeting his needs, and Setting up the environment for success, Charlie learned in four days a behavior that usually takes much longer to master.

CAPTURING THE CHOICE POINT: A FORMULA FOR SUCCESS

The simple yet important strategy of 'Capturing a dog's Choice Point' is the secret to why Charlie was able to create calm and repeat the desired behavior so quickly.

Simple Steps for Success

Step 1: I connected with him and met his needs.

Step 2: I captured the moment in time when he **chose** to lay down. 'The Choice Point.'

Step 3: I did not say a word or express any emotion when he chose to run around. I remained neutral.

Step 4: I did not **lure** him to lay down.

TIP: When you lure a dog to do something, they are not paying attention to their behavior. They are so focused on the lure that it takes lots of repetition for them to connect their behavior to their actions. When you deliver the treat **after** they make the CHOICE, learning happens very quickly with fewer repetitions.

When you recognize the power of CHOICE and the magnitude of learning available when you acknowledge that moment of CHOICE, the possibilities are endless. When you allow your dog the freedom to choose as much of his life as possible and immediately CAPTURE the CHOICE that aligns with your training goals learning happens very quickly. When dogs understand that their choices affect their lives, training becomes a series of communication between the two of you and it is a whole lot of fun! Your dog builds confidence because you celebrated their actions and *captured* a choice you want, a behavior they already perform on their own.

Interacting in this way helps your pup realize they have a choice and that their choices make a difference in their lives. As you consistently Capture the Choice Points, you propel learning exponentially. Your dog recognizes his inherent ability to learn which builds a solid foundation for more elaborate behaviors. Life becomes one gigantic party while your pup learns life skills to navigate the human world.

CHOICE AS A SKILL

Capture and Choice are incredibly connected. Our goal is to make the process of the dog making a choice and us responding to that choice as natural and automatic as possible.

This method of teaching enhances your dog's ability to navigate life in the human world and learn their job effectively. It becomes a series of interactions without the drama of scolding and punishment. Instead, it is a series of powerful 'YES' moments that teach your dog manners and life skills needed to thrive in the human world!

Notice and acknowledge behaviors you want to see repeated. Pay attention when your pup makes a choice you like and be prepared to Capture it by giving them something they desire such as treats, connection, touching, playing a good game of tug, or all of the above. Over time, the acknowledged behaviors will become an automatic way of navigating life in the human world.

PRACTICE: DOWN/STAY

In the previous chapter, we learned how to teach Calm as a Default Behavior. When any dog learns how to choose calm behavior in challenging situations it becomes a valuable life skill. In stressful moments the 'Calm' becomes the default behavior they rely on to bring themselves to a quieter, calmer state.

TIP: I teach dogs the automatic behaviors, i.e.: 'Calm as a Default' first, before teaching them on cue. What I discovered is that if you begin giving commands immediately, the dog will wait on the next command rather than moving through life choosing the correct behavior.

The following Practice is designed to build upon the strong foundations of CALM AS A DEFAULT. It is the method that I used to teach Down/Stay to my search and rescue dog, Piper after we spectacularly failed the mock test one month prior to testing.

I recommend that you build your skill in CALM AS A DEFAULT prior to teaching Down/Stay. Calm is a necessary skill to successfully navigating the human world. If it is not reliable prior to teaching the following Practice of Down/Stay, you risk losing the *automatic* Calm you practiced in the previous chapter. For service dogs and working dogs, the ability to calm themselves in hectic environments is a necessary skill.

Life skill: Teaching the 'Down/Stay' means to have the ability to tell your dog "lie down" and "stay" in one place and know that they will not move until you return to them. It allows you the ability to leave your dog in one place when you have to pass the

FEMA Disaster Assessment or if life calls you away unexpectedly.

This method of teaching the Down/Stay initially relies upon the dog's choice and your acknowledgment of that choice, while connecting their actions with the word DOWN. When you incorporate choice while teaching a behavior, learning happens very quickly.

I encourage you to practice the DOWN/STAY briefly and frequently in a variety of environments, but only use it in emergency situations until you are 100% sure it is solid. Overuse will result in losing the Calm as a Default and your pup will start to depend on you to tell him what to do in all situations, instead of calming himself automatically.

Puzzle Pieces for Success

Puzzle Piece 1: Train in short increments. Keep it very easy and attainable.

Puzzle Piece 2: NEVER call your dog from the requested Down/Stay. Maintain the expectation that you will **ALWAYS** return to them before releasing them from their position. (If you are going to call you dog, use a different word like 'Wait.')

Puzzle Piece 3: Release your dog while they are quiet, attentive and engaged. Celebrate the success and Go Play!

Supplies: A dog on a leash whose needs have been met (play time, bathroom time and exercise time), small treats and a patient human.

Putting the Pieces Together

Beginning level
Begin in a low distraction environment such as a quiet room in your home, or a similar place with nothing going on around you.

Step 1: Stand with your dog on leash beside you. Allow enough slack in the leash for them to stand, sit or lie down beside you but no more. (You are limiting their Environment by keeping them on a short leash.)

Step 2: Wait! Be patient, they will choose to lie down. Do NOT engage with them at all.

Step 3: When they choose to lie down, place a couple of treats between their paws on the floor.
    TIP: If the dog stands up before you place the treats between their paws, return the treats to your pocket. Say nothing and do nothing other than stand up and put the treats back in your pocket. Repeat steps 1–3 until you get the response you want and are able to reward them with the treats on the floor. Capturing the behavior the first time requires the most stealth. After the first time, the dog understands that if they remain, they receive treats, if they move, they get nothing.

Step 4: As soon as your pup eats the treats, say 'Let's Go,' and walk around a bit or take a 'Play Break.'

Step 5: Repeat steps 1–4 until your pup lies down quickly and looks up to you expectantly for a treat.

Step 6: Take a Play Break! Keep expectations easily achievable in the beginning. SUCCESS in every step along the way is the goal.

Connecting the word – 'Down'

Step 1: Stand with your pup on a leash. (I like to continue in the same environment for this step as well.)

Step 2: As soon as the dog chooses to lie down say, "Down" and place a treat on the ground between their paws.

Step 3: As soon as your pup eats the treats say, "Let's Go" and move around.

Step 4: Repeat steps 1–3 several times.

Step 5: Take a Play Break!

TIP: Repeat the Beginning Level and Connecting the Word 'Down' when you take a walk and your dog immediately lies down. CONNECT the word while the dog is in the Down position. At this beginning stage remember to communicate your appreciation 100% of the time by rewarding with treats and releasing with a, 'Let's Go' very quickly. Keep it short. Keep it successful!

Intermediate Level

You are ready to move to the Intermediate Level when your dog lies down as soon as you say, "Down." Begin this level in the same environment you used for the beginning level.

Step 1: Tell your dog to lie down, place multiple small treats on the floor.

Step 2: While the dog is eating the treats, turn around so you're standing directly in front of them.

Step 3: Immediately move back into position beside them and drop a few more treats.

Step 4: As soon as they finish eating the treats say, "Let's Go" and walk around together.

Step 5: Repeat steps 1–4 several times.

Step 6: Take a Play Break.

    TIP: This step happens very quickly and is the beginning of teaching your pup that even though you are moving, they need to remain in place.

Mastery Level: Phase I
You are ready to move on to the Mastery Level Phase I when you have the ability to say "Down," and move in front of them while they remain calm and relaxed. Your dog simply looks up at you with the expectation you will return and provide treats on the floor.

Step 1: While on leash, ask your dog to "Down" then place treats between their paws.

Step 2: Turn around facing them, place more treats between their paws.

Step 3: Take 1 step backwards and immediately 1 step forwards.

Step 4: Place more treats on the floor.

Step 5: Move back into position beside your dog.

Step 6: Release them with a 'Let's Go' and take a Play Break!

TIP: The goal is for the dog to stay in position 100% of the time while you move around. If the dog NEVER moves while you move, you have set the expectation that when you say "Down," they remain where you placed them until you return.

*If they follow you at any point, gently take them by the collar back to where you originally placed them and move through the steps a little slower ensuring you dog understands his job.

Mastery Level: Phase II

Move to this Phase only when your dog is consistent in Mastery Level: Phase I

Step 1: Ask your dog to "Down" Place treats between their paws.

Step 2: Turn around facing them, place more treats between their paws.

Step 3: Take 2 steps backwards and immediately 2 steps forward.

Step 4: Place more treats on the floor.

Step 5: Move back into position beside your dog.

Step 6: Repeat steps 1–5 increasing distance one step at a time.

TIP: Keep your practice sessions very short and successful. *STOP when you have the quiet position you desire.* End on a spectacular relaxed down. When you end while your dog is in a very quiet state, you once again have CAPTURED the quiet, emphatically saying, "YES!" You are doing exactly what I need you to do and now we will do what you want to do which is go play. This series of stopping while they are calm sets them up to continue the behavior in the future.

Step 7: Go Play with your pup, he has worked hard. Thinking is difficult.

TIP: You will reach a solid Down/Stay faster if you move slowly through the steps. If your dog moves toward you at any point, take them back to where you originally left them and start over at the last successful level. If they move again, go back to the beginning and move through all steps slowly to ensure understanding.

Mastery Level: Phase III – Adding Distractions, Duration and Distance

Do NOT move to this Level until you have super reliability at ALL previous levels. It is better to progress slowly through the levels with a solid understanding than it is to move quickly and continually have to go back to repeat the previous level.

Now we will add Distractions, Distance and Duration one at a time. These additions help you develop consistency, reliability and trust in your Down/Stay regardless of what is going on in the environment.

- DISTRACTION means to change the environment, move to a different location or use the same location and allow other humans, dogs, or toys into the mix. Distractions are anything that changes the current environment even a little bit.
- DISTANCE is where you are in relation to your pup. How far away you can go and your dog remain steady? At this level, it is vital you keep your slow and steady learning pace. Baby steps will take you farther faster than having to repeat previous levels, because you moved through the steps too quickly.
- DURATION is the time you leave your dog in the down position before returning. Again, progress slowly. 100% success is your goal. (Do NOT walk off and forget that you left your dog in a Down/Stay! Don't laugh, it has happened to some of us.)

TIP: Only change ONE thing at a time, if you change the Distance, do not change the location (Distractions) as well. If you change the Distractions, keep your Distance and Duration the same as previously successful.

Step 1: Add new and challenging environments and different locations. ONE AT A TIME!

Step 2: Move through all previous levels as slow or as quickly as your dog demonstrates success. At this stage, some dogs generalize very quickly and some need to complete EVERY step along the way each time you change a Distraction, Distance or Duration.

Step 3: If at any point your dog follows you, take them back to where you originally place them and then go back to the previous level of success.

Step 4: Continue to change the game as your dog demonstrates mastery during each change of Distraction, Duration and Distance.

Step 5: I REPEAT! Change only ONE component at a time.

TIP: The goal is: 100% SUCCESS AT REMAINING IN PLACE during each level advancement. Practice for a few minutes daily or multiple times daily. Have fun with it! Always end the session on a quiet, relaxed down. Then play, play, play. Have fun!

MAGGIE: CONNECTING WORDS TO ACTIONS

When Maggie was small, I offered her a cookie (treat) each time she went to her kennel as I said, "Maggie, do you want a cookie?" she trotted into her kennel to receive her treat.

I then said, "Kennel up" connecting the words "kennel up" with her going into her kennel. Time passed with this routine until she was much older and one day I said, "Kennel up," thinking she would go into her kennel. Instead Maggie just stared at me. I waited, giving her time to think. She didn't move.

I said, "Do you want a cookie?" And she went right into her kennel.

I figured out that I had taught her that "Do you want a cookie?" To her means 'go to your kennel.'

To this day, if I say, "Do you want a cookie?" she happily trots straight into her kennel with or without the cookie in my hand.

LINKING WORDS TO ACTIONS

The spoken word means very little to a dog until we link the word to their current action. If you said the word 'jump' every time your dog sat, to that dog, 'jump' means sit on your bottom. Words only have meaning to dogs when we connect them to actions in the present moment.

As you move through your daily life with your dog, link words you plan to use for their current action by saying them *during* the behavior.

Dogs understand so much more than we give them credit for. Use this natural ability your dog already possesses to teach them many different words. Label your actions and their actions.

As you prepare their dinner say, "Are you hungry?" before long they will pick up on the words even if you're not preparing dinner. As you fill their water bowl, say, "Are you thirsty" as you fill their water bowl. As you walk to the door, ask them, "Do you want to go outside?"

When you label your dog's actions in everyday life, they become fluent in the spoken language. The only limit will be how much you want them to know? When you have to spell out words while talking to your partner, maybe you have taught them too much!

PRACTICE: GET BUSY (GO TO THE BATHROOM)

Life skill "Get Busy" means to go to the bathroom. Using the bathroom when requested is an awesome skill when traveling or when the weather is less than ideal.

Puzzle Piece for Success

Piece 1: Say the words the moment the dog is using the bathroom.

Piece 2: Do something fun after.

Piece 3: Pay attention to the signs you need to take your dog outside.

Putting the Pieces Together

Step 1: Say the words "Get busy" in a normal tone of voice one time while your dog is in the act of using the bathroom.

Step 2: Quietly deliver a treat when they are finished while telling them good job.

Step 3: Now go do something FUN!

Step 4: Repeat each time your dog goes to the bathroom!

TIP: It's very important in the early learning stages to do something fun AFTER they use the bathroom. Take a walk, play, or simply allow more outside sniffing time. If you take them immediately back inside when they finish, your dog will connect going to the bathroom with going inside prematurely – outside fun time is over. The dogs will hold it until they have had their fun and sniff time.

*By this time, you are beginning to recognize how your choices affect your dog's behavior. Good job!

Mastery Level

Step 1: When you are in a hurry, simply go outside and say, "Get busy." Your pup will immediately take care of business quickly.

TIP: When your dog has the 'Get busy' firmly in their knowledge base, they will give you a sign they do not need to go. Some dogs will come back, sit in front of you and stare at you if they are finished. Acknowledge this action and it will become routine.

CAPTURE THE DESIRED BEHAVIORS & CONNECT THE WORDS

A few behaviors I like to Capture on a regular basis are:

- A service puppy in training standing facing backwards when I stop. Link the words: "Watch my six."
- A service puppy standing behind me in the store. "Block"
- If you have a search dog, capture the bark!
- If you have a detection dog, capture the sit.
- Walking nicely beside me on a leash. "Heel"

- Greetings with four paws on the floor. "Off"
- Anytime they choose to look at me. "Look"
- Quiet in the kennel before I open the door.
- Calm while indoors.
- Sitting or lying down when I stop (either off leash or on.)

You can use these ideas and create your own CAPTURE list. And to create your list of words you want your pup to know. The opportunities to celebrate your dog being good are endless. The more consistently we notice them doing what we want them to do and rewarding them with an emphatic 'YES,' the more quickly they learn and the more fun you both have along the way. By Capturing the beginning behaviors you want, you will be able to build them into the precise behaviors you need for your dog's chosen job.

As you master the Capture, the next lessons of Ignore, Interrupt, Replace and Reset will be easy to implement and will further amplify your dog's ability to learn quickly and efficiently.

CHAPTER 6

IGNORE, INTERRUPT, REPLACE & RESET

"Dogs should be allowed as much liberty as they can responsibly handle. The greatest gift of training is that it increases a dog's ability to handle liberty."

– Chad Mackin

As you continue to practice using the Puzzle Pieces of **Connection, Meeting Needs, Regulating their Environment**, and now **Capture**, the puzzle pieces you'll learn in this chapter will help you naturally begin to communicate boundaries that limit unwanted behavior while encouraging desired behaviors.

The strategies we'll be covering in this section are a necessary for the teaching process. Because let's face it, sometimes you have to mitigate behaviors and tell your dog that is not how we are going to behave.

IGNORE, INTERRUPT, REPLACE and RESET

In this chapter, you will learn when, why and how to IGNORE behaviors that are not useful. Dogs like to be connected and engaged with you. Choosing to not engage with them is a powerful learning strategy.

You will learn how to INTERRUPT unwanted behaviors and either REPLACE them with actions you want to see or RESET them and allow another opportunity to choose very quickly. These methods teach your dog the behavior they were engaged is not acceptable and they can 'do this,' (the behavior you have chosen) instead or simply stop what they are currently doing. Once you learn and begin implementing these Puzzle Pieces, you will notice difference in your dog's behavior almost instantly. You are capitalizing on your dog's 'Choice Point,' responding with another option which communicates clearly exactly which behavior is acceptable and which behavior is not.

Implementing ALL of these Puzzle Pieces increases learning incredibly fast.

PIPER DROPS THE BALL

One day as I was working on my computer, Piper came into my office, carrying a ball. She walked up to my desk and dropped it in my lap. It was her attempt to lure me outside. I must have been in a mood to procrastinate as it didn't take much convincing on my part. I stopped my work and joined her outside for a some fun.

Later that same day, I was reading a book, when Piper, once again brought me a ball; and once again, I stopped what I was doing and joined her outside. It wasn't until later that I realized that I set up a chain of behaviors that would create challenges down the road.

I had created a situation that Piper took full advantage of. Anytime she noticed me sitting down anywhere for more than five minutes, she took that to mean I was 'available for playtime.' My responses to her taught her that when she brought me a ball, I would stop whatever I was doing and join her for a game.

This was a new routine I had to quickly alter or I'd risk ending up with a dog that didn't have boundaries and would pester me constantly.

The next time Piper dropped a ball into my lap, I placed it on the floor. Piper picked it up and dropped in into my lap a second time. Instead of following her outside as I had before, I told her, "I'm not playing right now." And put the ball back on the floor.

We had created a new game. Piper was excited about this

new version of play and tossed the balled once again into my lap. For her, this was almost as much fun as going outside to play for real. It didn't help that John sat in his chair and laughed, knowing I just got sucked into Piper's new pastime.

My solution to solve this new problem was to pick up all of the balls up off the floor and put them where she couldn't reach them. This didn't dissuade Piper at all, she just started dropping any toy she could find into my lap. This time, I didn't take the bait.

I realized in that moment I had to completely rethink my strategy, because Piper is smart and creative, she could and would find many ways to get me to do whatever she wanted.

I decided to implement the IGNORE technique. Simply put, I ignored her, I did not even look at her. Piper responded with a bark showing her disapproval of my new approach of 'zero attention,' but I stayed committed to the IGNORE. It took some time, because Piper is a very persistent dog, but Ignoring her worked.

In addition to IGNORING the unwanted behavior, whenever Piper chose to go lie down, when she chose the 'calm,' I CAPTURED the desired behavior. I acknowledged and celebrated it by inviting her outside to play ball while she was in a calm, quiet state not bothering me.

Over time and with some consistent practice, Piper began to realize I was not going to engage with her whenever she dropped something on my lap. She learned that the interaction she desired only happened when she chose to be calm. As soon as she made this desired choice, I rewarded her with a some fun. Eventually she realized the quickest way to get to go outside and play, was to choose 'Calm as her default' behavior.

Piper is a dog who never gives up, which is an awesome

quality for a canine involved in search and rescue of the missing or buried under rubble. But teaching her the manners and life skills for us to peacefully coexist took some time to master. Even at twelve years old, I'm not sure we have mastered it yet!

Each moment is unique, but ultimately her behavior of CALM is the goal. She doesn't always get the reward of going outside when she is quiet, but she appreciates those moments of play when they are offered.

Over time, and with consistency, CALM is now Piper's default behavior, which is what helps her manage her own energy moment to moment.

IGNORE: THE ART OF DOING NOTHING

Dogs love interaction with their humans and learn very quickly how to engage us in their games. For the IGNORE principle to work, you must cease to be a point of focus and interaction for your dog. You become still, you stop talking and stop making eye contact. You become a like a statue.

In this position of 'nothingness,' you must wait for the dog to change their behavior, for them to do something different before responding to them. At first, they will be surprised or confused by this lack of response from you and they WILL try a different behavior to get you to engage, sometimes even barking at you. Remain steady. It does work!

When the dog attempts a different behavior, respond by giving them feedback, telling them "YES." CAPTURE the preferred behavior by letting them know their current choice of action is one to be repeated. Ultimately you want these preferred behaviors to grow into life skills and manners to help them navigate the human world more smoothly.

The Ignore technique is very simple, but does take repeated practice to be effective, especially if you have a persistent pup like Piper. It takes time for the dog to figure out the unwanted behaviors will get them nothing. But the desired behaviors will give them a response they like. Be patient and maintain your own calm. Time, practice and patience are your friends in this situation.

With consistency, you'll begin to see the actions you take today grow into excellent manners and life skills tomorrow.

PRACTICE: LOOSE LEASH WALKING

Life skill: This practice helps you refine the skill of your dog walking nicely beside you while on a leash. The leash needs to have some slack in it rather than being taut. It is designed to help your dog walk easily by your side instead of pulling you along.

Puzzle Pieces for Success

Piece 1: Offer treats along the seam of your pants, down the side of your leg where you want the dog to walk. (Where you give the most treats is the location your dog will want to hang out.)

Piece 2: Before you begin, engage with your pup. Enjoy a Play Break! This engages them with you making you their focus.

Piece 3: Start in an environment with little to no distractions. For example, your living room when it's quiet.

Supplies: A dog on a leash, treats in a treat pouch or easily accessed pocket, a favorite toy, and an engaged human.

Putting the Pieces Together

Beginning Level: Limited Distractions

Step 1: Attach the leash and with treats in your pocket, take a few steps.

Step 2: Feed treats on the side you want your dog to walk almost continually at first.

Step 3: If your pup is not focused on you and acting a little crazy, freeze, IGNORE and wait. Simply give them a moment. When they 'check in' with you, acknowledge the 'check in' and begin walking again.

TIP: If you begin each walk with your pup acting crazy for the first few steps, you are rehearsing the crazy rather than the practicing walking nicely.

Step 4: Acknowledge them while they are walking beside you with touches, verbal interaction, and treats. In the beginning, continual interaction and CAPTURING them walking nicely is imperative.

Step 5: After a few successful steps, give them permission to "Go sniff or Follow their Nose." (By giving them what they want, you are further reinforcing their awesome behavior of walking nicely beside you.)

REMEMBER: When your dog chooses to pull or keep the leash tight, you choose to IGNORE, freeze and do nothing until he makes the choice to allow slack in the leash. (They do NOT have to come all the way back to you!)

TIP: By giving your dog permission to engage in one of their favorite activities, you meet their need to sniff the ground, relaying the message that 'if you do what I want, you get to do what you want.' Over time, the process of your pup walking beside you will become automatic and effortless, because they know you will provide many opportunities to do the things they love to do.

Step 6: Walk a few steps with your dog beside you. While your dog is walking, attach the words to the actions. Say "Heel" or "Walk with me" connecting words to your dog's correct position by your side.

Step 7: Repeat Steps 2–6 increasing the distance as your dog is successful.

*Start small and grow the behavior as you pup becomes more proficient.

SOMETIMES, LESS IS MORE

It is more important to walk 10 steps with the dog beside you and focused on you, than it is to walk around the entire block constantly trying to get their attention.

When you begin in very small increments, you create smaller pockets of success which gives you a solid foundation for longer more enjoyable walks in the future. This sets you and your pup up for frequent, short but successful rehearsals, rather that longer practices that perpetuate unwanted behaviors.

Remember to acknowledge them when they do well, and always end the practice session when they are walking nicely beside you. Allowing play time when they are walking nicely beside you further encourages the behavior of walking nicely, because you gave them permission to play or sniff while they are engaged with you and doing what you desire. You once again CAPTURED the behavior you desired. When they choose to pull, you choose to IGNORE and become a statue. When they choose to keep slack in the leash, you give them what they want, moving forward, sniff time or play time.

As things continue to go well on your daily walk, gradually add more distance.

The practice of 'Loose Leash Walking,' helps our dogs to learn that:

- If and when they pull = WE STOP
- When they don't pull = WE GO

MORE ENCOURAGEMENT FOR WALKING BESIDE YOU

When you meet your dog's needs before they have to advocate for themselves, you set up an environment of cooperation and your dog learns that you will frequently allow time for him to do 'dog stuff.'

Methods to encourage Connection and Meet their Needs while they are correctly walking with you are:

- Allow them to stop for a good sniff by giving them permission to, "Go sniff."
- Invite them to pause for a 'Play Break.'
- Acknowledge when your dog chooses to 'Check In' and immediately give them permission to continue what they were doing. When you immediately give permission to go back to what they were doing, this encourages the 'Check in' even more.
- The power of giving your dog Permission to do what they already want creates long lasting positive impact on your dog's behavior.

LOOSE LEASH WALKING: Intermediate Level

Puzzle Pieces for Success

Piece 1: No Rehearsals of pulling on the leash. Do **NOT** keep walking when your pup chooses to pull.

Piece 2: Meet their needs with a 'Discovery Walk,' allowing engagement with the environment through sniffing.

Piece 3: Stop regularly for 'Play Breaks.' Meet their needs!

Putting the Pieces Together

Intermediate Level: Move Locations and Practice

Step 1: Move to a different location and build on the steps at the beginning level, increasing the distance as your success allows.

TIP: Remember to stop and play or allow sniffing while your dog is walking nicely. When they demonstrate the desired behavior of walking nicely on the loose leash and you acknowledge it, you 'Capture the Behavior' of walking nicely. A behavior rewarded today is one that will be repeated tomorrow.

Step 2: When the dog chooses to walk in front of you and pulls, FREEZE, do not move. Remain silent and give them time to realize you are going nowhere until they are beside you. ALLOW THEM THE TIME TO THINK, process and make a choice.

Step 3: When they *choose* to create slack in the leash, walk and count to 3 before dispensing treats.

Step 4: As you progress, increase the distance you walk nicely together before dispensing treats.

Step 5: Practice noticing distractions before your dog does and be proactive in focusing their attention on you.

Mastery Level: High Distractions and Long Enjoyable Walks

Step 1: Continue building on the Beginning and Intermediate Levels, increasing distance in small increments. Practice daily on short, easy walks gradually increasing distance as you are successful at the shorter distances.

Step 2: Change locations, build skills by going to more distracting environments.

Step 3: Practice engaging your dog with clicks, sounds and words in addition to treats. (Making a variety of sounds with your voice is another method of gaining your dog's attention.)

Step 4: Be exciting! Be the best thing in your dog's world. At this level, you can be the 'source of fun,' and all you will need is your leash and the willingness to engage!

TIP: Don't move to this level too quickly. Dogs need time, practice, and success to master this skill. Connection is the Puzzle Piece that shines during a great Loose Leash Walk!

REMEMBER: Loose leash walking is another skill that improves as you practice correctly. Simply walking will not get you where you want to be with loose leash walking if your pup is pulling most of the time. As you rehearse walking on a loose leash, your pup's skills will improve very quickly.

INTERRUPT AND REPLACE OR INTERRUPT AND RESET

INTERRUPT and REPLACE or INTERRUPT and RESET is a communication practice that when applied consistently is a very effective teacher.

INTERRUPTING is precisely what the word implies, not allowing the pup to continue his current undesirable behavior. The Interruption is completed with neutral emotion from you, rather than because you are angry at their current behavior. You are simply giving information that their current behavior is not acceptable. The goal with INTERRUPT is for the dog to recognize what works for them, what doesn't work for them and to develop the ability to regulate themselves without you having to constantly monitor their behavior.

There are two ways to interrupt behavior:

1. Physically: is exactly what it says. If the dog is staring down a squirrel, another dog or a human, you simply step in front of them. If your dog is small, pick them up and gently stroke them. You are using your body to prevent them from engaging in the current behavior, thus INTERRUPTING the behavior they are engaged in.

2. Using a Variety of Sounds: Interrupting with your voice, squeakers or clickers is very effective to distract them from

unwanted behaviors. Interrupting with sound is a quick and effective way of distracting them, which creates an opportunity for you to change your dog's focus and provide another option for them. Either REPLACING their unwanted behavior or RESETTING them when appropriate.

REPLACE happens when you offer the dog an acceptable behavior that prevents them from immediately returning to the original unwanted one. (THIS IS A VERY IMPORTANT STEP. Do not skip it!)

Replacing the undesired behavior with a different desired behavior is vital to the success of this method. If all you do is INTERRUPT the behavior, but you don't give the dog something else to do, the dog will immediately return to the previous undesired conduct. The goal is to provide something the pup enjoys doing *instead* of the current unwanted action.

REPLACE tells them, "Hey, this way of behaving is not okay, try this way instead." By offering an acceptable action to replace the unacceptable one, you communicate, "Chewing on my shoe is *not* okay, but chewing on this bone *is* okay." You effectively show them how to behave and what you want.

RESET is a follow up to INTERRUPTING when there is not an acceptable replacement behavior that's easy to offer. RESET is exactly what it says, it tells the pup that their behavior is not okay and you are going to prevent it. It gives them an alternative, i.e. watching from inside the kennel rather than being close to me. Using RESET is just a simple time out and it works beautifully, because you respond to the dog's choices and give them opportunities to make different choices very quickly.

For example: When I'm cooking and young puppies put their paws on the cabinets trying to get closer to the yummy smells, I pick them up with neutral emotion and gently place them in a nearby kennel for a few seconds (literally less than a minute the first time.) I go back to my cooking, then pretty quickly walk back to them and let them out of the kennel, giving them another opportunity immediately to choose a desired behavior. If they go back to the counter and put their paws up again, I repeat the process of picking them up and placing them in the kennel. This time, I give them two or three minutes before I let them out.

This process usually takes only two or three repetitions for them to realize that if their paws go up, they have to watch me cook from their kennel and if they keep their paws on the floor, they can be near me. Which is one of the most important things to a dog, being near their human.

The goal is to teach dogs how to *choose* acceptable behaviors for themselves; to set them up so they can make choices that benefit them. They can and will self-regulate and develop confidence to learn very quickly what behavior works well and what behavior does not get them what they want.

PETE BEING HYPER FOCUSED

Pete is a beautiful little Goldendoodle puppy who absolutely loves people and enjoys lots of interaction, especially with strangers he meets on walks. The problem is that when he is with David, his person, they can't even make it down a street in a peaceful way, because Pete pulls on the leash to get to other walkers.

On these walks, Pete grows hyper focused and 'stares down' any person who might be approaching and then pulls and jerks his dad toward them. This strategy for Pete to get attention isn't pleasant for David or anyone else they may encounter on their path.

In a situation like this, we needed to Interrupt Pete before he began pulling. So my plan to alter this behavior was to Interrupt Pete's pattern with plenty of 'loaded sounds,' like clicks, smooches, or squeaks before he started pulling.

These sounds encouraged Pete to change his focus away from the stranger and back toward David. The moment Pete looked at David, he was rewarded with treats, play and interaction.

David INTERRUPTED Pete's stare with a sound and REPLACED the stare with a meaningful interaction with him. Thus meeting Pete's need for an abundance of human attention while creating a beneficial behavior at the same time.

PRACTICE: INTERRUPT & REPLACE OR INTERRUPT & RESET

Life skill: The process of Interrupting and Replacing, when done correctly, tells the pup two things:
1. This behavior is not okay.
2. But this other behavior is acceptable.

Through this process dogs learn which behaviors are valuable and worthy of repeating and which ones aren't. This practice also provides the ability to redirect your pup during stressful situations allowing you to move away quickly if necessary.

Load a variety of sounds

One of the easiest ways to Interrupt your pup is with Sound. In order to do this, you need multiple sounds and words 'loaded.' Loaded means to have these words connected with a fantastic reward, so when you make the loaded Sound, the dog immediately turns his attention to you.

Ideas for sounds: The words, Nice!, YES!, pup-pup-pup (in a high-pitched voice), smooches, squeakers in your pocket, clickers, a whistle etc. Use a variety of sounds that are easy to make. Change up sounds frequently to prevent overuse of one sound, rendering it ineffective. Utilizing different sounds also helps to keep your pup engaged.

Puzzle Pieces for LOADING Success

Piece 1: Load one sound at a time in one session.

Piece 2: Connect the sound with a treat. (Or play.)

Piece 3: Do not pay attention to the behavior your dog is engaged in unless he's barking. If he is barking, wait until he is quiet before you continue, or you'll risk capturing the bark and encouraging the dog to bark more.

Supplies: A dog on a leash, small, easily consumed, highly valued treats, a human ready to respond quickly. (If your pup is not treat motivated, use play to engage with them when you make the sounds.)

Putting the Pieces Together

Loading signals

Step 1: Make the sound you have chosen.

Step 2: Give a treat.

Step 3: Make the same sound.

Step 4: Deliver the treat.

Step 5: Repeat steps 1–4 quickly one right after another.

You know the sound is loaded when you make the sound

while your dog's attention is focused elsewhere, and the dog stops what he is doing and looks at you.

Testing the sound: Take a walk in a familiar area and make the sound. Does your pup stop what they are doing and look at you? If so, you are ready to continue. If not, get better treats and practice in a less distracting environment. Then test again.

REPLACE

For the INTERRUPT and REPLACE method to be successful, another behavior needs to be provided. Give the pup something to do that prevents him from immediately going back to the interrupted behavior.

Puzzle Pieces for Success

Piece 1: Get creative with the alternative behaviors.

Piece 2: Mix it up, use a variety of signals, words and actions to interrupt.

Piece 3: When you have nothing to offer, REALLY ENGAGE with your dog. Think Play Break with yourself as the toy!

TIP: There are times that you will walk out the door with, no treats or toys in your pockets. In those moments, be fun embodied. Think of a child's energy when opening a present and create it within yourself. I promise, your dog will focus on you rather than any distractions that may appear in the environment.

Putting the Puzzle Together

Step 1: When your dog is engaged in an undesirable behavior, make the 'loaded' sound.

Step 2: Immediately provide a treat then offer the alternative behavior. (If treats aren't available, take off running and say, "Let's get a treat!" I promise, your dog will follow.

Step 3: Take a Play Break. Sometimes it is acceptable to use the Play Breaks as your alternative behavior.

Ideas for Optional Behaviors:

- Pet them with their paws on the floor rather than anywhere on you.
- Play 'Find it' (below) to give them something to focus on rather than the environment.
- Interact with them after interrupting the bark.
- Offer a toy or play tug rather than focusing on "squirrels" in the environment.
- Turn around and jog away quickly, encouraging your dog to keep pace with you.
- Give them something acceptable to chew rather than furniture or socks.
- Be 'more fun than dirt' and engage with them.

Be creative and find alternative behaviors your dog loves. Maintain engagement with you as you soar to the top of your dog's fun list. Alternative behaviors look different for each dog. Capitalize on whatever your dog loves.

RESET

Use RESET when there is not another acceptable behavior or when you need to teach the pup not to do something, i.e. Put their paws up on the counter. The RESET is simple teaching technique that says, "You are not going to do that and if you do, I'm going to let you spend a little time in the kennel." When I do not have a kennel available, I use the leash as my Reset helper or my car.

For example; when we are hiking off leash and the pup repeatedly gets too far away, I just keep them on a leash for a short time. But very quickly I let them have another opportunity to stay close by. This technique capitalizes on the dog's great choices which empowers them to make better choices.

Another example of a RESET: As the dog gets out of the car, he immediately begins barking or lunging. Simply pick them up and place them back in the car for a brief minute. Try getting them out again pretty quickly. What is their response? You may have to repeat a couple of times until they figure it out.

When using the RESET part of this method, keep is short and very quickly give them an opportunity to make another choice. Repeat the RESET if their choice is the same undesired behavior as previously and allow them a few minutes rather than a few seconds in the 'time out.'

I've discovered that dogs who are trained utilizing these methods learn very quickly that their behavior affects their life and they figure out how to adjust their behavior to get them what they want.

PRACTICE: FIND IT

Life skill: This practice increases focus on the human and meets the dog's needs to sniff. Practice with this game provides an *optional* behavior for the Interrupt and Replace technique. By the time the pup has finished the game, the distraction is no longer important, and the pup has shifted his focus to you.

Puzzle Pieces for Success

Pieces 1: Practice on a rug rather than on slick floors to prevent the treats from rolling too far and the dog from slipping around in their haste to get them.

Piece 2: Hold a handful of treats waist high in front of you.

Piece 3: In the beginning, allow the dog to see where you dropped the treat.

Putting the Puzzle Together

Beginning Level
Starting the Game: Show the dog the treats in your hand. Ask, "Do you want to play Find It?"

Step 1: While your pup watches, drop a treat on the floor near your feet.

Step 2: Say the words "Find It" with your dog sniffing the floor for the treat you just dropped. These first 2 steps are completed almost simultaneously.

Step 3: When the pup looks back to you expectantly, repeat steps 1 and 2 several times.

Step 4: Take a Play Break. (For some dogs, this is so exciting, it becomes the Play Break.)

Intermediate Level: Part I
Move to this level when your dog demonstrates proficiency by immediately starting to sniff when you tell them to, "Find It!"

Putting the Puzzle Together

Step 1: Warm up by playing the Beginning Level of Find It first.

Step 2: Toss the treats first to the Right and say, "Find It!"

Step 3: When they come back and look at you, toss the treat to the left and say, "Find It!"

Step 4: Take a break and go for a walk.

Intermediate Level: Part II

Step 1: Warm up by repeating steps 1–3 in the Intermediate Level: Part I

Step 2: Gently grasp your dog's collar.

Step 3: Toss the treat while your dog is watching.

Step 4: Pause for a second or two, before letting go and say, "Find it!" At this point, your pup knows the game and pulls to go after the treat!

Step 5: Repeat a couple of times and take a Play Break.

Step 6: Move the game to a new location. Repeat the Beginning Level, then move through the steps of the Intermediate Levels. This usually happens very quickly now the dog knows and loves this game.

TIP: I like to move around and keep the dog on his toes and focused on me and the treats in my hands. At this point, 'Find It' becomes your 'Play Break.'

Mastery Level: Part I
Your dog demonstrates understanding when you say, "Find It" randomly and your dog immediately drops his nose to the floor searching for a treat.

Piece 1: Change locations and make sure you have a door to limit access to a different area.

Piece 2: Warm up with the intermediate level of 'Find It.'

Piece 3: If your dog needs a little help on this step, show them with your hand how to look for the treat you tossed out the door.

Putting the Puzzle Together

Step 1: Close the door to limit access to the next 'Find It' area.

Step 2: While the pup watches, open the door a little and drop a treat close to the door, but out of their line of sight.

Step 3: Immediately open the door and say, 'Find it!'

Step 4: After the dog finds the treat, bring them back behind the closed door. (At this point, I usually drop more than one treat.)

Step 5: Repeat steps 1– 4 a few times, gradually increasing the distance you toss the treats, creating more challenge.

Mastery Level: Part II

Step 1: Secure your dog in another room so he/she cannot see where you hide several treats in your new 'Find It' area.

Step 2: Retrieve your dog and say, "Find it!" Allow them time to use their nose to sniff out the treats.

Step 3: If they miss some, use your hand gliding along the floor to give them a hint.

Step 4: Be creative and have fun surprising your dog with Find It!

Change it Up: Show your pup his favorite toy and play the game with toys rather than treats. When they retrieve their favorite toy, enjoy a game of tug.

Finish the game by taking a walk and enjoy the increased focus in your pup.

MODIFY YOUR DOG'S BEHAVIOR

When Ignore, Interrupt, Replace, and Reset become a part of your daily life, it becomes a method of communication, interaction and responding to the dog's actions that allow you to stay calm and refocus your dog. You are able to modify their behavior without scolding or drama, giving them clear communication as to what works and what doesn't work for them.

Remaining neutral while teaching is an integral piece when applying these methods effectively. Over time it becomes a simple matter of quickly and calmly responding to them with either a "YES," that is exactly the behavior I'm looking for. Or That's not what is wanted, try this instead (provide an optional behavior). Or I'm going to let you hang out with me for a few minutes when they really want loose to play or run.

When you approach training in this manner, it frees your dog to make choices without the negative fallout and creates a relaxed environment for learning. The choices, both positive and not so great, your pup makes are simply information to help you adjust your training and set up the environment for success and better learning. The pup makes a choice, we make a choice, back and forth as we teach life skills and manners to navigate this crazy human world. The dog figures out very quickly how his choices affect what happens in his life.

Successfully implementing Ignore, Interrupt, Replace and Reset takes practice, because you must teach yourself how to respond to the behaviors your dog engages in, while 'checking your emotions at the door.' Dogs do not do things to merely frustrate you, they do what has worked in the past. You're learning how to make split second decisions and then handing it back to your dog and allowing them to make another choice. It becomes like a conversation with a friend where you both have input, and each are listening and responding to one another.

As we move into the next chapter, RECALL, you'll continue to utilize each of the three foundational Puzzle Pieces of CONNECTION, MEETING YOUR DOG'S NEEDS and REGULATING THE ENVIRONMENT.

Now with the additional puzzle pieces of CAPTURE, IGNORE, INTERRUPT, REPLACE and RESET in your repertoire, you will incorporate all of them when learning how to create an amazing RECALL.

CHAPTER 7

RECALL

"Recall is the completed Puzzle."

- Sharon Dilley

By now, I hope you've created some time to implement and practice the ideas, techniques and methods you have read in The Puppy Puzzle. I imagine you are already noticing your brilliant dog demonstrating better manners and life skills, adjusting their own behavior just a little as they figure out which behaviors work for them and which ones don't.

Learning to master any skill takes time and practice. The goal with the Puzzle Pieces I've outlined in this book is to make them simple and effective so you can easily incorporate them into your current training program. Over time these practices will expand your partnership and enhance communication with your dog; ultimately creating a lifelong impact on their behavior and how they navigate the human world, maximizing their potential in their chosen jobs.

When all of the pieces fit together as completed Puzzle, we can move forward in creating a solid RECALL.

The RECALL you have on your dog is the sum of all the Puzzle Pieces!

AN EXERCISE IN TRUST

Recall is more than a word connecting a specific behavior to an action performed by the dog. It is bigger than a cue that demands immediate obedience. When a strong RECALL is needed, the dog is out of reach, not on a leash and has complete *free will to choose* whether or not to listen to you.

RECALL is an exercise in TRUST that you have firmly established in your partnership.

REMEMBER: Connection + Meeting their Needs + Regulating the Environment = An amazing RECALL!

As you begin practicing with Recall, ask yourself three questions to be certain you have the necessary foundation in place:

1. Have you developed the CONNECTION with your dog to the point that he *chooses* you?

2. Have you MET YOUR DOG'S NEEDS to the point he *trusts* you and does not have to advocate for himself?

3. Have you set up the ENVIRONMENT for *success* and practiced with few distractions?

Every single interaction you have with your dog is either encouraging your RECALL or discouraging your RECALL. Read that again: Every interaction with your dog is either building a better RECALL or tearing down your RECALL.

Some of the actions on your part that will destroy your dog's desire to come immediately are:

- Scolding him for **any** reason when he arrives.
- Telling him to sit after he comes quickly to you. (You just missed your opportunity to CAPTURE your dog's incredible recall.) Instead, you Captured a great sit.
- Not Meeting your dog's needs of running, sniffing or simply playing outside.
- Poisoning their name and recall word, by repeating it too many times or using it in a harsh manner.
- Increasing the distractions too quickly before you have practiced enough when coming to you is easy.
- Only calling your dog when it is something they don't

like, effectively becoming the one who ends ALL fun.
- Calling them repeatedly when they ignore you. (If you really need them, keep quiet, walk to them and attach the leash.)

PIPER, KALI & GABRIEL: NAVIGATING THE SNAKES

A strong Recall can save your dog's life. When it is firmly in place, we know without a doubt that our dog will choose us, over anything else.

Piper, Kali and six-month old Gabriel were outside for the last time before bed. They were enjoying some playtime before coming in for the evening. It was dusk, a little later than usual when I stepped to the door to call them.

I immediately noticed a copperhead snake slithering toward the back door and heading straight into the path of the carefree trio.

"COME!" I called in a high-pitched voice as I encouraged them to run faster.

Thankfully all three ran to the door so fast the snake didn't have time to react or strike.

Piper, Kali and I spent many hours building the Trust for a great RECALL. They recognized the urgency in my voice and responded immediately. Gabriel, as a young pup new to our family did not yet have the training, but simply followed the older dogs to the safety of the house.

Our time practicing paid off in what could have been a very dangerous situation. The time you invest in each of the three foundational Puzzle Pieces develops TRUST, which leads to a great RECALL, that can literally save your dog's life.

I've had experiences in working with my dogs, where I've

discouraged my RECALL as well. As I'll share in this next story...

MAGGIE: CAN'T CATCH ME

When Maggie was very young, I had several other young puppies training to be service dogs at the same time. I had too many puppies for only one person to Meet their Needs which is vital to building the TRUST leading to a great recall.

One particularly busy week, I let the puppies out of their play area, but didn't provide them with the amount of time I normally would to 'Meet their Needs' for free time out of the back yard. This included Maggie, and after a short amount of time, I called her back to me so I could allow someone else out to play for their brief time.

She ignored me, stood about fifteen feet away and just stared at me. Maggie effectively said, "NO! I'm not coming inside, I'm not done, I haven't been outside long enough." I took a step toward her and she took a step away. I tried again. I took another step toward her, and she took a step back. I attempted to sweet talk her into allowing me to catch her to take her back into the house, but she was having no part of it.

I knew in that moment the problem wasn't with Maggie; the failure was mine. She wasn't being stubborn or obstinate, she was communicating with me. I hadn't done my job of 'Meeting her Needs' in a way that encouraged her TRUST me. In this moment, Maggie was forced to advocate for herself. I had not told her with my actions that she would be released for more free time soon.

I effectively set up the environment for Maggie to choose not to come. I created a scenario where she felt she had to **advocate** for herself, because I did not allow her time to sniff and explore, a basic 'dog need.' In this scenario, Maggie was choosing to make sure she had more time to play, because I did not provide it the last time she was released.

In the days that followed, I set up the environment for all of the pups, especially Maggie to have more than enough free time to run and play outside. We played until they **choose** to come inside. And I did NOT call her name until she was already coming toward me, letting me know she was finished playing.

Within a week, she was better. By the end of a month with her need to play until her heart's content met, she consistently came when I called. I met her needs and she no longer had to advocate for herself. Her trust in me was restored and the RECALL issue corrected.

Recently, I let Maggie out for some time to run and play when I spotted a delivery driver speeding up the driveway toward our house. I immediately called her to me even though I had just opened the door to her freedom. She ran to me very quickly!

TRUST had been restored; her RECALL was incredibly effective. As soon as the package was delivered and the delivery truck out of sight, I released her and allowed her freedom to continue. TRUST is at the center of your dog's RECALL. As the level of your dog's TRUST in you strengthens, your ability to RECALL your dog will improve.

PREPARE FOR AN AMAZING RECALL

ALL of our practices are built on the three foundational pieces of The Puppy Puzzle. In order to develop an awesome RECALL,

we will add a couple more components.
1. CONNECTION: Be the BEST thing in your dog's life.
2. MEET YOUR DOG'S NEEDS: Everyday! All the time!
3. Set up the ENVIRONMENT FOR SUCCESS.
4. **PERFECT PRACTICE.** Zero Rehearsals of Not Coming. If you are not 100% certain your dog is going to come when you call, do NOT utter a word. Stay silent and go to them.
5. **CAPTURE** the Moment Your Dog Chooses to Come! Generate enthusiasm in your voice and by your actions.

PERFECT PRACTICE – EVERY TIME

We have spent a significant amount of time on Connection, Meeting Your Dog's Needs, and Regulating the Environment. What does that look like when it comes to creating a great recall?

Connection or lack of it permeates every aspect of your Recall. Make sure you have spent plenty of time on this first Puzzle Piece before actively working on this section. Even re-read the Connection Chapter if you want. Meeting Your Dog's Needs is a daily routine. Establish that before this. Regulating the Environment is one of the initial Puzzle Pieces we will set up very carefully in this Chapter.

This section addresses the Puzzle Piece of setting up the environment for success every single time. The goal is to support your dog with as few distractions as possible in the beginning. When you provide success in the beginning, it builds upon itself.

Adding **Perfect Practice** to the first three Puzzle Pieces will enhance your RECALL practice.

Perfect Practice means: You are 100% sure your pup is going to come to you before you say a single word. By implementing perfect practice, you *rehearse* correctly every single time when coming to you is easy. You want there to be no doubt about what your recall word means and ZERO rehearsals of NOT coming when called. When there is no doubt in your dog's mind about the meaning of your recall word and when you have practiced until it becomes muscle memory, your dog is more likely to come when the stakes are high and returning to you immediately is crucial.

There are many fun ways to incorporate Perfect Practice into your daily RECALL routine:

- Practice when your dog is already heading your way.
- Practice when you're 3 feet from them and holding a favorite toy.
- Practice inside.
- Practice outside after they have time to exercise when they are ready for a drink and immediately give them *permission* to continue their play.
- Take off running down the hallway and call them. They will chase you!
- Practice when you are anywhere, and you notice them coming to you.
- Practice anytime, anywhere and all the time as long as you set up the environment for 100% success and make it **FUN** for your pup the second they arrive.
- Have a friend hold your pup around the chest, run away, and call them. (This creates desire to get to you.) When they pull toward you, your friend lets go.

CAPTURE THE RETURN

One of the most powerful methods to integrate the learning is to CAPTURE the precise behavior you desire the *exact* moment it takes place. Split second timing of rewards is even more important for the RECALL practice. The goal is to CAPTURE the **moment** your dog heads toward you with an excited "YES!" And the **moment** they arrive by becoming 'more fun than dirt.' Play with them, give them treats and do whatever they love.

There is an element to Capturing the Recall to be aware of. Many times, people call their dog. The dog performs a beautiful RECALL, running to them quickly. When the dog arrives, they immediately tell the dog to SIT.

The moment you told the dog to SIT, you *missed* the opportunity to Capture the Recall. In that moment, you rewarded the SIT, not the RECALL. Basically, you have communicated "Yes! Great Sit." Not, "YES! Great RECALL!" Remember, dogs live in the present moment, not in the moment that happened a few seconds ago.

When I call a dog, I begin the celebration as soon as they start moving toward me. I generate excitement with my voice and my energy. In addition, I squat down, further encouraging them to come to me quickly.

When they arrive, I grasp their collar and dispense treats freely. I celebrate with them. If I have a toy, we play. If I have nothing, I become the toy. I am FUN embodied! This is the acknowledgment for a job well done. I become 'more fun than the dirt they were sniffing!'

Many times, I surprise them by letting go of their collar immediately after they arrive, giving them permission to go have more fun which further encourages them to come the next time I call. Remember, your dog chooses to come or not to come next time, because of your actions this time.

12 PIECES FOR A PERFECT RECALL

Building a strong foundation is paramount for RECALL to become a reliable life skill. Incorporate the following pieces into your daily life as much as possible. The more you practice when there is nothing at stake, the better your recall when the stakes are high.

- **Capture**. Celebrate, acknowledge, and reward when your dog chooses to start your way and when he arrives.
- **Connect** the action of running to you with your recall word. When your dog is a couple of steps away from you and running toward you say, "(the dog's name) and your recall word" in a happy voice. Your recall word needs to be UNIQUE and ONLY used for calling your dog to you.
- **Acknowledge** the behavior you want to see again. The behavior of running to you is the behavior you want your dog to repeat.
- **Do NOT scold** your dog when they choose to come! (No matter what they have done.) If you do, they will stop coming when you call.
- **Do NOT take anything** from your dog when they choose to come. Either allow them to carry whatever they have in their mouth or trade them for something *more* valuable.
- **Do NOT be the Fun Killer.** This damages a recall more quickly than you can imagine. Stopping fun can be as simple as taking them inside or leaving the park. To the dog, that makes

you the one who ended their great time.
- **NEVER** chase your dog! If they do not want you to catch them, you won't. If you choose to play this game in your backyard where it's safe, your dog may choose to play this game if he gets loose on a busy highway.
- **Grasp** your dog's collar and then give a treat, when your dog returns to you. Reach for their collar first and THEN bring out the treat. This gets them accustomed to you reaching for their collar anytime, not just when treats are present.
- **Sit or lie down** if it's imperative they come quickly for their safety. This unique action from you will grab their attention and they will almost always choose to come and investigate what you are doing. When they arrive, play, play, play.
- **Practice calling** your dog when they are already heading your way. Grasp their collar, give a treat and release them immediately giving them **permission** to continue their fun! *Permissions are POWERFUL!*
- **Do NOT poison your dog's name or recall word** by repeating the words too often or saying them in an angry voice. Keep both your dog's name and recall word *special and happy*. The goal is for them to equate their name and recall word with good things EVERY single time they hear it!
- **Set your dog up for 100% SUCCESS** each step along the way. If you increase the difficulty and your dog chooses not to come, go back to the previous step and keep practicing with fewer distractions until you build a stronger recall.

Incorporating the 12 Puzzle Pieces for a reliable recall into your daily life will create a greater level of TRUST between you and your dog. As you move forward with the following Practice: 'Recall in Action,' those pieces along with the three foundational Puzzle Pieces will be the Puzzle Pieces to build a super recall!

PRACTICE: RECALL IN ACTION

Life skill: RECALL is the behavior of your dog returning to you quickly when you call. Your dog needs to come close enough for you to reach their collar. A solid recall is a testimony of an incredible relationship and the TRUST between you. When you have a great recall, you have the ability to manage the environment when your dog is off leash, ensure their safety and protect them from dangers they do not even realize exist.

Connection + Meeting Needs + Regulating the Environment = an Amazing RECALL!

Puzzle Pieces for Success

Piece 1: Begin in an environment where success is 100% attainable.

Piece 2: Capture the action every time your dog chooses to return to you!

Pieces 3: Practice perfectly. Zero rehearsals of not coming.

Supplies: A dog who TRUSTS you, an engaged handler, treats, toys and the willingness to 'be more fun than dirt!'

Putting the Puzzle Pieces Together

Beginning Level: Use Connection and Meeting their Needs
Set up a distraction free environment, a hallway or an empty room with no other animals or people around. REMEMBER: The smallest behavior that you want can be built into the amazing final behavior you desire.

Step 1: Sit down on the floor or a low stool or crouch down.

Step 2: When the dog notices you and starts coming toward you, say your dog's name and your recall word **ONE** time.

Step 3: Celebrate and Capture the desired behavior. Dispense multiple treats at a time while telling them how awesome they are. Or play a game of tug.

Step 4: If they choose not to come, move quickly in the opposite direction. Do NOT call them again but celebrate with them when they choose to follow you!

    TIP: If they choose not to come, go back to the 12 Pieces for a Perfect Recall and continue strengthening each piece before attempting this step again. And be sure you 'meet their needs.' Set your dog up for success at each interval along the way.

Step 5: When steps 1–4 are consistently successful, call them when they are NOT already coming toward you.

Step 6: Watch for their Choice Point (the moment they choose you over what they are currently doing) and CAPTURE the behavior by saying "YES!" that is exactly what I need from you further encouraging them even more. Squat down and meet them at their level. Or start a game of chase by running away. They will catch up to you and LOVE IT!

Intermediate Level: Expanding the Environment
You are ready for the Intermediate Level when your dog is consistent and reliable with the Beginning Level. It's better to move through the levels slowly than it is to move quickly only to realize the foundation was not strong enough and you have to go back and begin again.

Move to a different Location, outside with them on a long leash. The leash (12 to 20 foot) will allow more freedom to roam and move further away from you, while keeping them safely connected.

Step 1: Allow the dog to freely move away from you while still attached to the leash.

Step 2: As soon as your dog 'Checks In,' say, "*Dog's name* and your *recall word*."

Step 3: Squat down to encourage them to run to you.

Step 4: Celebrate their choice to run to you and the **moment** of arrival!

Step 5: When they arrive, grasp their collar and give them a treat or several treats, which encourages them to come all the way to you. And RELEASE them, giving permission to go play again!

REMEMBER: Permissions are POWERFUL and releasing them immediately is POWERFUL!

Step 6: If the dog happens to choose to go the other way or does not return to you, turn and run away from them. The dog's chase drive will kick in and they will follow. Celebrate when they catch up to you!

Step 7: After you grasp their collar, immediately let go and say excitedly, "Go PLAY!" you have just become even better by giving them *permission* to continue having fun!

Step 8: Practice steps 1–7 several times. Then skip waiting for the 'Check in.' Call them when they are engaged with the environment, sniffing or looking around. Do they stop what they are doing and come? If so, you have succeeded in building your RECALL. If not, go back a few steps and make sure you have practiced regularly ALL '12 Pieces for RECALL Success,' consistently met their needs and the first 7 steps in this Practice.

TIP: Practice in a variety different locations so the action of them running to you immediately, becomes automatic.

Mastery level: Distractions – Bring on the Challenge!

You are ready for the Mastery Level when your dog comes to you, even when they are engaged with the environment. No matter what enticing smells they may be noticing around them, they stop what they are doing and return to you in several different scenarios and locations.

TIP: In the beginning, ALWAYS give them permission to continue doing what they were doing after they come when you called. This further solidifies your position of being the FUN rather than the fun killer.

To practice at this level, you need a secure place for your dog to be off leash to run around freely.

Step 1: Take them off the leash. One of the biggest changes to the environment you can make is to remove your physical attachment to them. When the leash is gone, the TRUST you have built with them is your security. You will know pretty quickly if you have built the great foundation or need a little more practice.

TIP: When you take them off the leash for the first time, allow them plenty of time to play, run around and expend some energy before calling them. When they do return to you, immediately release them by telling them to, 'Go Play!' This builds in the TRUST that you are going to meet their needs *especially* when they come when called.

Step 2: Add distractions and level of difficulty slowly over time. Remember when adding distractions and level of difficulty only change one thing at a time. Allow your pup to be successful, then add something different.

Step 3: Challenge your dog! As your proficiency grows stronger, up the stakes in ways that are fun. But still maintain safety. This is how you CREATE an amazing RECALL!

PERFECT PRACTICE CREATES AN AWESOME RECALL

If you find that your Recall is lacking and your dog routinely chooses to keep doing whatever it is that he is doing, instead of running to you, continue to practice the 12 Pieces for a Perfect Recall. Notice how you are implementing the three foundational Puzzle Pieces of Connection, Meeting Your Dog's Needs and Regulating the Environment. Which Puzzle Piece is missing or not as strong as the others? Focus on that and keep working on it. RECALL will improve as you continue building the TRUST between you.

The goal is **100% success** at each level of RECALL practice. The option of not coming is not an option!

As your success continues at each level of difficulty, the chance of your dog not coming to you when you call is reduced, providing you both with a sense of security that when you need an awesome recall your dog will come running! In an important moment, your dog will instantly come running in response.

I encourage you to use every opportunity to practice your RECALL. It will become a life skill that provides you and your dog with a degree of flexibility and freedom to navigate a wide variety of situations with confidence.

There truly is no better feeling than knowing your connection is so strong, that it takes a single word to guarantee an immediate and happy return to your side.

CONCLUSION

WRAPPING IT ALL UP

"Dogs have a way of finding people who need them and filling an emptiness we didn't know we had."

– Thom Jones

As our time together comes to a close, your time with your pup is just beginning. The pieces we have put together in the pages of The Puppy Puzzle have the capacity to positively impact every aspect of your life with your dog.

If you have welcomed a new puppy into your environment, the pieces of The Puppy Puzzle will prepare you to learn and grow together. The techniques you have discovered will help them navigate the 'strange, new place' that is your home. When you make it your priority to give them your time, your Connection will grow. When you Meet their Needs, they no longer have to advocate for themselves. And when you Regulate their Environment, they grow confident in you and your relationship. You will see your young dog move quickly from 'Surviving mode to Thriving mode.'

If you have a more mature dog, one who already possess some necessary skills for navigating the world or has already achieved some success in their chosen job, you now possess the knowledge to help them excel. With the pieces of the Puppy Puzzle on your daily schedule, you will invite greater confidence and encourage them to reach their maximum potential.

And if you have a senior dog, the pieces of the puzzle will help them feel peaceful and content as they age.

The 3 pieces of The Puppy Puzzle:

- CONNECTION
- MEETING THEIR NEEDS
- REGULATING THEIR ENVIRONMENT

Will serve and support any dog at any age, whether they are a beloved family member, an athlete, a search and rescue dog, detection dog, therapy dog, or a service dog.

A RETURN ON YOUR INVESTMENT

I invite you to go out into the world and practice. If you mess up, no big deal, simply make a different choice or set up training in a different way to ensure success. Implement one or two of the Puzzle Pieces and notice the impact on your training. Put the entire Puzzle together and watch your dog soar.

The magnitude of positive influence the Puzzle Pieces have on you and your pup directly corresponds to the time you invest in them. If you want to see wonderful changes in your life with your dog, consistently apply the individual pieces of the puzzle presented here and make them a daily habit.

Notice the changes that evolve over time. Pay attention to the subtle differences that begin to show up in the beginning and then the incredible differences that emerge after a few weeks of applying these principles.

You'll notice that your dog who previously had zero or very little recall begins coming when you call his name. You'll notice the dog who used to jump up and put their paws all over you, now eagerly waits for you with all four feet on the floor. And, the dog who never settled now practices Calm as a Default behavior, relaxing with you more often.

If you compete in agility with your dog, you'll notice that split second edge, because the communication between you is improved. If you have a working dog, you'll notice they have more stamina or are just a little bit better at their job. You'll notice them becoming sharper and more in tune with what you need from them, which creates a better understanding and greater ability to complete their jobs with confidence and grow into their maximum potential.

Connection + Meeting Needs + Regulating the Environment = TRUST!

THE REWARD OF AN AMAZING RELATIONSHIP

A firefighter I once trained with said to me, "Your dog knows more than you when they are out there searching. Learn to read your dog and work with your dog to find the missing, the buried under the rubble."

I believe we are only beginning to unlock the potential of dogs. We sell them short because they don't communicate in the same way we do. But they absolutely know more than we give them credit for.

It all comes down to what kind of relationship you desire. Do you want a partner, friend and ally? Or do you want a dog who obeys every command and waits for you to tell him or her the next move to make? Or maybe a little bit of both?

Dogs possess so much wisdom and are incredibly willing to share it. When you choose to walk through life beside your pup, two-way learning and communication occurs naturally. Once you start giving, you will be amazed at what you get back.

We learn the most when we are open to new and different ideas. It is my intention that all of the practices I've shared with you in The Puppy Puzzle will help you and your dog develop a partnership, that makes all things possible!

I invite you to learn from some of the successes and mistakes

I have shared with you within these pages. I encourage you to take your time and view every interaction with your dog as an opportunity to grow. But most importantly, I encourage you ***TO HAVE FUN!***

I wish you and your pup all of the health, happiness and success in the world. It has been an honor to be of assistance to you on your journey in your adventures together.

Now... Enjoy the Journey!